Communication Is a Game.

Be a Pro.

A Complete Training Manual for Structured Thinking, Confident Speaking, and Real-World Influence

Author: Shivam Nanda.

This book will not comfort you.
It will train you.

Some concepts discussed in this book are inspired by communication training frameworks taught by Vinh Giang. The concept of Love Languages referenced in this book was originally developed by Dr Gary Chapman in his book *The 5 Love Languages*.

First Edition

Author: Shivam Nanda

PREFACE

I created this book after observing a consistent pattern in students, college learners, and young professionals. Many of them were intelligent. They understood concepts clearly in their minds. They could solve problems, analyse situations, and generate ideas. Yet when it came to expressing those ideas aloud, something broke.

Their sentences became scattered. Their voices lost strength. Their breathing became shallow. Their thoughts moved faster than their clarity. Some rushed. Some froze. Some avoided speaking altogether.

The problem was never intelligence.

The problem was a lack of structured communication training.

In school, we are trained to write answers and solve equations. We are trained to memorise definitions and prepare for exams. But we are rarely trained to think in structure, control our breath, use our voice intentionally, or tell a story with purpose.

Communication is treated as a personality trait — something you either have or do not have. This belief is incorrect. Communication is not personality. It is not fluency, It is not speed, It is not talent. It is a trainable system.

Your thoughts require structure, your voice requires breath control, your body requires alignment, your fear requires understanding, your influence requires storytelling, and your relationships require emotional intelligence.

If one of these elements is weak, expression suffers.

Most communication advice is incomplete. Some books focus only on vocabulary. Others focus only on confidence. Some speak about body language. Others speak about storytelling. Rarely do they combine thinking structure, physiology, delivery mechanics, influence, and emotional awareness into one coherent system.

This book does. It is not a motivational book, not a collection of speaking tips, not a personality development manual. It is a structured training program in written form.

Inside this book, you will learn why your voice shakes, why you run out of breath, why you rush sentences, and why filler words dominate your speech. You will learn frameworks that organise your thoughts instantly. You will train your voice like an instrument. You will understand how storytelling influences perception. And in the advanced section, you will explore how people interpret communication differently through emotional patterns.

This book demands participation. Reading will give you awareness, but practice will give you skill. Communication is not speaking, it's being understood — clearly, confidently, and intentionally.

And being understood requires discipline.

INTRODUCTION

This Book Is a Training System

Most people believe communication means speaking good English.

That belief is incomplete.

You can speak fluent English and still be unclear, use advanced vocabulary and still fail to be understood, speak fast and still say nothing meaningful.

Communication is not about how much you speak, It is about how clearly you are understood.

Many students and young professionals struggle not because they lack knowledge, but because they lack structure. Their thoughts are scattered, breath is unstable, voice lacks control, fear interrupts clarity and body sends mixed signals. And because no one ever trained them properly, they assume something is wrong with their personality. Nothing is wrong with your personality. What is missing is training.

Communication is a system built on three pillars:

1. Structured Thinking
2. Physiological Control
3. Deliberate Practice

If your thinking is unclear, your sentences will be unclear. If your breathing collapses, your voice collapses. If you never practice intentionally, how to use pause and tone intentionally

- How to structure answers using frameworks
- How to use storytelling effectively
- How emotional perception influences communication

- How to follow a 30-day mastery protocol

This is not a motivational book.

It will not ask you to “just be confident”, not give you random tips and not promise an overnight transformation. Instead, it will demand effort.

You will record yourself, audit your speech, train your breath, practice structured thinking and repeat drills. If you complete the exercises seriously, improvement is not optional — it is inevitable. But if you only read and do nothing, nothing will change.

This book is for students, graduates, and young professionals who are ready to take communication seriously. It is for those who are willing to move from awareness to application.

Knowledge is power. Wrong: Let's correct it: “Applied knowledge is real power.” And communication becomes powerful only when practised.

Turn the page with intention.

TABLE OF CONTENTS

Where Are You Right Now?

Do this assessment twice.

Once now — before you read a single chapter, before you attempt a single exercise. Your honest score today is your baseline. It is not a judgment. It is a starting point.

Then again on Day 30 of the protocol at the back of this book — after every chapter, every exercise, every day of deliberate practice. The difference between those two numbers is your proof. Not someone else's result. Yours.

Rate yourself honestly from 1 to 5 on each statement below. 1 means this is rarely true for you. 5 means this is consistently true for you right now. No one is watching. Be accurate, not optimistic.

A — Clarity and Structured Thinking
(Chapters 3 and 4)

When asked an unexpected question, I can organise my thoughts and answer clearly without rambling.
1 □ · 2 □ · 3 □ · 4 □ · 5 □

My answers have a clear beginning, middle, and end rather than a stream of unconnected thoughts.
1 □ · 2 □ · 3 □ · 4 □ · 5 □

I can explain a complex idea simply without losing the other person halfway through.
1 □ · 2 □ · 3 □ · 4 □ · 5 □

I lead with my main point rather than slowly building toward it and hoping the listener follows.

1 □ · 2 □ · 3 □ · 4 □ · 5 □

Section A Total: ___ / 20

B — Voice, Breath and Delivery

(Chapters 5, 6, 7 and 8)

My voice stays steady and controlled even when I am nervous or under pressure.

1 □ · 2 □ · 3 □ · 4 □ · 5 □

I vary my pace and pitch to hold attention rather than speaking in a single flat tone throughout.

1 □ · 2 □ · 3 □ · 4 □ · 5 □

I use pause deliberately rather than filling every silence with filler words or rushing to the next sentence.

1 □ · 2 □ · 3 □ · 4 □ · 5 □

My breathing supports my speaking — I do not run out of breath mid-sentence or gasp between thoughts.

1 □ · 2 □ · 3 □ · 4 □ · 5 □

Section B Total: ___ / 20

C — Physical Presence and Body Language
(Chapters 9 and 10)

My posture is open and grounded when I speak — not collapsed inward or restless under pressure.
1 ☐ · 2 ☐ · 3 ☐ · 4 ☐ · 5 ☐

My gestures are intentional and controlled rather than nervous, scattered, or directed at my own body.
1 ☐ · 2 ☐ · 3 ☐ · 4 ☐ · 5 ☐

I maintain natural, confident eye contact without staring uncomfortably or breaking away constantly.
1 ☐ · 2 ☐ · 3 ☐ · 4 ☐ · 5 ☐

My facial expression reflects what I am saying — it does not stay flat, contradict my words, or perform an emotion I do not feel.
1 ☐ · 2 ☐ · 3 ☐ · 4 ☐ · 5 ☐

Section C Total: ___ / 20

D — Storytelling and Influence
(Chapters 11 and 12)

When I tell a story, people stay engaged — they do not lose interest, check their phone, or glaze over halfway through.
1 ☐ · 2 ☐ · 3 ☐ · 4 ☐ · 5 ☐

My stories have a clear point — they do not simply describe what happened and leave the listener wondering why it mattered.
1 ☐ · 2 ☐ · 3 ☐ · 4 ☐ · 5 ☐

I can tell a compelling story in under two minutes without losing the tension or the key moment.

1 ☐ · 2 ☐ · 3 ☐ · 4 ☐ · 5 ☐

I use specific sensory detail that makes the listener feel present in the moment rather than vague general descriptions.

1 ☐ · 2 ☐ · 3 ☐ · 4 ☐ · 5 ☐

Section D Total: ___ / 20

E — Emotional Intelligence and Listening
(Chapters 13, 14 and 15)

I can sense the emotional state of someone I am speaking to and adjust my approach without being asked to.

1 ☐ · 2 ☐ · 3 ☐ · 4 ☐ · 5 ☐

People feel genuinely heard after talking to me — not just acknowledged, moved along, or managed.

1 ☐ · 2 ☐ · 3 ☐ · 4 ☐ · 5 ☐

I notice when my own body language or tone contradicts what I am saying — and I can correct it in real time.

1 ☐ · 2 ☐ · 3 ☐ · 4 ☐ · 5 ☐

I can navigate a difficult or emotionally charged conversation without becoming defensive, shutting down, or saying something I regret.

1 ☐ · 2 ☐ · 3 ☐ · 4 ☐ · 5 ☐

Section E Total: ___ / 20

Your Total Score: ___ / 100

Write this number down. Write today's date next to it. Do not change it later — your first honest answer is the only one that matters here.

Then come back on Day 30 and do this again.

What your score means today:

80 to 100 — Strong foundation. You are not starting from zero. Focus on depth, consistency, and the areas where you dropped points. The gap between good and exceptional is where this book lives.

60 to 79 — Developing. You have clear gaps and you probably already know what they are. The exercises in this book are designed to target exactly those gaps. Keep going.

40 to 59 — Stage Two. You are aware enough to see the distance between where you are and where you want to be. That awareness is not discouraging — it is the beginning of every real improvement. The discomfort you feel right now is the signal that rewiring is already starting.

Below 40 — This is your starting point. Nothing more, nothing less. The size of the gap is simply the size of the opportunity. Every communicator you admire started somewhere. This is where you start.

One final instruction before you turn the page. Do not go back and change your answers after reading more of the book. The score you gave yourself before you knew more is the most accurate measure of where you actually are. Protect it. It is the only version of this assessment that belongs entirely to you.

How to Use This Book

This is not a book you read and set aside. It is a training manual, which means it works only when you work with it.

Rule 1 — Read in order the first time. Each part builds on the one before it. Part I resets how you think about communication. Parts II and III build the internal foundation. Parts IV through VI develop your external delivery. Part VII deepens your intelligence. Do not skip ahead on your first read.

Rule 2 — Do every exercise without exception. Every chapter ends with a practical drill. These exercises are not optional extras. They are the point. Reading about communication does not build communication skills. Doing the exercise does. If you skip the drills, you are reading theory. That is not what this book is for.

Rule 3 — Record yourself regularly. The self-audit process described in Chapter 2 and the 30-Day Protocol requires you to record yourself on video. This is uncomfortable. Do it anyway. The recording reveals what you cannot see from inside your own experience. It is the most honest feedback tool available to you, and it costs nothing.

Rule 4 — Use the 30-Day Protocol as your training system. After reading all fifteen chapters, turn to Part VIII. Complete the baseline diagnosis first. Then follow the four-week structure. The protocol turns everything you have learned into an embodied habit — the kind that does not require conscious effort because it has become the way you naturally communicate.

Rule 5 — Return to Chapter 15 whenever you need answers. The final chapter answers the 24 most-asked questions about communication. Treat it as a reference. Return to specific questions as real situations arise — a difficult conversation, a presentation, a job interview, a moment of conflict.

This book is for you if you want to communicate with clarity and confidence and are willing to practice, record yourself, and stay with the discomfort of Stage 2 (What is Stage 2? You'll learn about this in the upcoming chapter).

This book is not for you if you are looking for quick tips and surface fixes. Real communication skills are not built through tricks. It is built through understanding and repetition. This book demands both.

PART I

RESET YOUR UNDERSTANDING

Every speaker you have ever admired started where you are now — completely misunderstanding the game. Not because they lacked talent, but because they had been taught the wrong definition.

They chased fluency when they needed clarity. They mistook speed for intelligence and rushed through ideas that deserved space. They treated confidence as a personality type — something you either have or you don't — and waited for it to arrive like a guest who never showed up. They believed introversion was a ceiling, and so they built their lives beneath it.

This section does not teach you to speak better; it teaches you to stop believing things that are making you worse. Communication is not performance. It is not vocabulary. It is not the absence of nervousness or the presence of a commanding voice. It is one thing and one thing only — the ability to make another person understand exactly what you mean. Every technique in this book is built on that definition. Until you accept it, nothing else will stick.

IS EVERYTHING YOU
KNOW WRONG?

CHAPTER 1

Communication Is Not Speaking

In a large technology company, a young engineer named Arjun was asked to present an idea to the leadership team. He had spent days preparing slides filled with impressive terminology. When the meeting began, he spoke quickly, using complex words and technical explanations. His sentences flowed smoothly, and he sounded confident. By the end of the presentation, he felt proud of how articulate he had been.

But when the meeting ended, the room remained quiet.

One of the senior managers finally asked, "So… what exactly are you proposing we do?"

Arjun paused. He had spoken for nearly ten minutes, yet the decision-makers still did not understand the core idea. His vocabulary had been advanced, his speech fluent, and his delivery energetic—but the message itself had never landed clearly.

A few weeks later, another engineer, Meera, presented a similar proposal. Her language was simple. She spoke slowly and structured her explanation around one clear problem and one clear solution. She did not try to impress the room. She focused on making sure everyone could follow her thinking step by step.

When she finished, the CEO immediately responded, "That makes sense. Let's move forward with it."

Both engineers were intelligent. Both had prepared carefully. The difference was not vocabulary, speed, or even confidence. The difference was clarity.

Arjun had been speaking. Meera had been understood.

And that difference reveals the real measure of communication. It is not how fluent you sound or how sophisticated your language appears. The true question is much simpler: after you finish speaking, does the other person understand your message exactly the way you intended? If they do not, then all the fluency, speed, and confidence in the world cannot replace clarity.

Before You Begin

Put your hand up if you have ever known exactly what you wanted to say — and said nothing.

Not because you lacked the knowledge. Not because the thought was unclear. But because something between the thought and the room stopped you. Maybe it was the fear of being wrong in front of others. Maybe it was the voice that asked what if I say it badly. Maybe it was simply the habit of staying quiet — practised so many times over so many years that it no longer felt like a choice. It just felt like who you are.

Here is what most people are never told.

It does not matter whether you are seventeen or forty-five. Whether you are in a classroom, a boardroom, a job interview, or a family dinner. The experience of having something worth saying and not being able to say it the way you mean it — that experience does not belong to any one age or stage of life. It belongs to almost everyone. The student who freezes during a presentation. The professional who goes silent in a meeting while a less-prepared colleague speaks confidently. The person who leaves every difficult conversation wishing they had said the thing they only found the words for on the way home.

What separates the people who communicate with clarity and confidence from those who do not is not talent. It is not personality. It is not some quality distributed unevenly at birth that some people simply received and others did not.

It is practice. Specific, structured, repeated practice — applied to a skill that almost no one is ever formally taught.

Your marks got you through school. Your qualifications got you through the door. But in every room that matters — the interview, the presentation, the negotiation, the conversation that could change something — what carries you forward is your ability to communicate what you know, what you feel, and what you believe in a way that another person can actually receive.

That ability is not fixed. It is not your personality. It is not your introversion or your accent or your background. It is a skill. And every skill that has ever been built was built the same way — through the decision to begin, followed by the willingness to be uncomfortable until the new thing becomes natural.

Every exercise in this book can be done with zero equipment, zero money, and no audience. A phone camera. A quiet room. Thirty minutes. That is the entire requirement.

The only thing standing between the version of you that stays silent and the version of you that the room listens to — is the decision to start.

You have already made it. You picked up this book.

Now let's start building it.

The Language Myth

Here is something I hear constantly from students: *"My English is weak — that's why I can't communicate."*

It sounds reasonable. It feels true. But in most cases, it simply isn't.

English is a language. Communication is a skill. And there is a significant difference between the two.

A language is a tool — like a hammer or a paintbrush. But owning a good brush does not make you a painter. What makes you a painter is knowing what you want to create and having the discipline to put it on the canvas. The same is true with communication. You can hold a rich vocabulary and still leave people confused. You can speak in plain, everyday words and still move an entire room.

The real gap most students face is not a language problem. It is a thinking problem. Unstructured thoughts, combined with the fear of being judged, create the illusion that the tool is broken — when the actual issue is that the builder hasn't yet learned to build.

Think about it this way: a carpenter does not wait for a perfect hammer before starting his first table. He picks up what he has and begins. With every joint he cuts and every nail he drives, he gets better — not because he upgraded his tools, but because he used them.

Communication works the same way. When your thoughts are organised, even simple words carry weight. When your thinking is scattered, even sophisticated language creates noise. Clarity does not come from vocabulary. It comes from structure — from knowing what you want to say, why it matters, and how to lead someone from where they are to where you want them to be.

The moment you stop waiting to be "fluent enough" and start speaking with what you already have, three things begin to happen. Your language improves through use. Your clarity improves through structure. Your confidence improves through repetition. The only thing that improves nothing — is avoidance.

One Practical Note on Learning a Second Language

If you are building fluency in English — or any language that is not your first — there is one shift that separates people who become genuinely fluent from people who remain perpetually intermediate, no matter how many years they study.

Stop translating. Start thinking.

I know this from the inside. English is my second language. Hindi is my first — and honestly, my favourite. It is the language I think in when I am with family, the language I laugh in, the language that feels most like home. I grew up switching between Hindi medium and English medium schools, which sounds like an advantage but created its own kind of confusion. I was never fully settled in either. In Hindi classrooms, I was fine. In English classrooms, I was translating — forming every thought in Hindi first, converting it, speaking it, then translating the response back. The loop was exhausting. And for a long time I convinced myself that this was simply what it meant to speak a second language. That the gap between Hindi and English in my head was permanent. That fluency was for people who had grown up in English-speaking homes.

Then I made one change. I stopped treating English as a subject and started treating it as a parallel language. Not a replacement for Hindi — I had no interest in that. But a second home in my mind. A room I could think in directly, without passing through translation first.

That shift changed everything.

Most learners approach a second language as a translation exercise. They think in their mother tongue, convert the thought into the second language, speak it, hear the response, translate it back, form a reply in their mother tongue, convert it again, and speak. This loop is exhausting, slow, and it keeps the second language permanently at a distance — always a tool being operated, never a voice being used.

The shift happens when you begin thinking directly in the language you are learning. Not translating into it. Thinking in it.

This feels impossible at first. It is not. It is a habit — and like every habit in this book, it is built through repetition rather than understanding.

Start small. When you wake up in the morning, name what you see around you in the second language. Not full sentences. Just words. The ceiling. The window. The light. When you are waiting for something, describe what is happening around you silently in the second language. When you are about to speak, resist the instinct to form the sentence in your mother tongue first. Let the second language reach for the thought directly — even if it reaches imperfectly.The mistakes you make while thinking in the language are not failures. They are the brain building new pathways. Every imperfect thought in a second language is a repetition that makes the next thought slightly more fluent.

The goal is not to eliminate your first language. Hindi will always be the language I reach for when I want to say something that needs to be felt rather than just understood. That will not change. The goal is simply to give the second language its own room in your mind — a room it can furnish over time with its own instincts, its own rhythms, and eventually its own voice.

Fluency is not the absence of an accent. It is not the abandonment of your mother tongue. It is the presence of thought in the language itself — the moment when you stop arriving at English through Hindi and simply arrive.

That moment is available to anyone willing to practise the journey.

The Speed Myth

In 1974, British television host David Frost sat across from Muhammad Ali in a widely watched interview and asked him what many considered the most personal question of his career.

"What would you like people to think about you when you are gone?"

Ali did not rush. He did not scramble. He let the question sit in the room for a moment — the kind of pause that most people fill with noise out of pure discomfort. And then, slowly and with complete deliberateness, he answered:

"I'd like for them to say he took a few cups of love, one tablespoon of patience, a teaspoon of generosity, one pint of kindness. He took one quart of laughter, one pinch of concern — and then he mixed willingness with happiness, added lots of faith, and stirred it up well. Then he spread it over a span of a lifetime — and he served it to every hungry person he met."

The room was silent when he finished. Not because the words were complicated. Because they arrived with the full weight of a man who had given them exactly the space they deserved.

Muhammad Ali was not just a boxer. He was one of the most powerful communicators of the twentieth century. But watch his interviews closely — not his punches, his *pauses*.

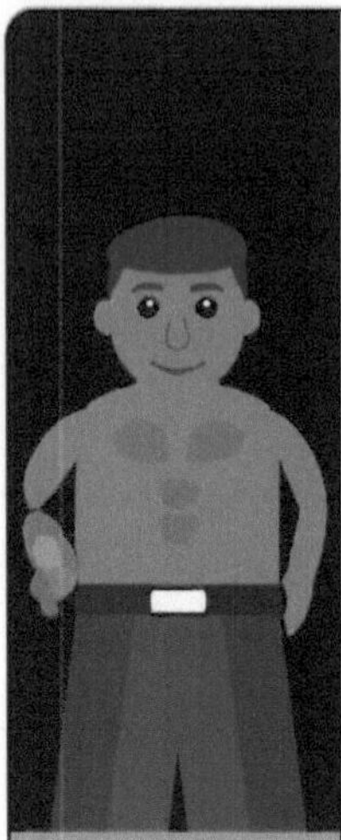

PERSONALITY PROFILE

Muhammad Ali

1942 – 2016 • United States

Three-time World Heavyweight Boxing Champion and one of the most recognised athletes in history. Ali was as celebrated for his words as his fists — his speeches, press conferences, and pre-fight proclamations were performances of controlled, deliberate communication that commanded every room he entered.

> **COMMUNICATION LESSON**
> *Ali understood that pace and pause were weapons.*
> *He never rushed. He let silence work before a sentence landed.*
> *The slowness of his delivery made every word feel inevitable.*

When a journalist tried to rattle him with a sharp question, Ali never scrambled for words. He would stop. Breathe. Let the silence sit in the room for a moment. And then, slowly and deliberately, he would deliver a single sentence that hit harder than any combination he ever threw in the ring. The world leaned in every time — not because he was fast, but because he was completely, almost dangerously, unhurried.

Now contrast that with something far more familiar.

Think of a student — let's call him Rajan — preparing for a job interview at a multinational firm. His first language is not English, and that fact sits in the back of his mind like a warning light he cannot switch off. He rehearses his answers until midnight. He tells himself: *just keep moving, don't stop, don't give them time to notice.*

In the interview room, the moment the first question lands, Rajan begins — and does not stop. Words arrive in a continuous stream. His sentences blur into each other. His hands move faster. His breathing grows thin and tight in his chest. He covers every point he prepared. He uses every phrase he rehearsed. He finishes in ninety seconds and looks up, hoping for approval.

The interviewer smiles patiently and says, "Could you slow down a little and walk me through that again?"

Rajan had not failed because his English was poor. His English was fine. He had failed because speed had swallowed his message whole.

This is what the Speed Myth costs you. When you rush into a second or third language, the intention behind it is understandable — you want to sound fluent, capable, and natural. But what the listener actually receives is the opposite signal. Rushing sounds like anxiety wearing a costume. And the body knows it too. When you speak too fast, your breath becomes shallow. When your breath becomes shallow, your voice loses its steadiness. When your voice loses its steadiness, your confidence drops further. And so you rush even more to compensate.

It becomes a loop that tightens with every sentence.

The antidote is not slower speech for the sake of it. It is *intentional* speech. Strong communicators treat pace the way a surgeon treats a scalpel — with precision and purpose. They move quickly through context and background. They slow down when the key idea arrives. They stop completely when they want something to be felt, not just heard. That pause — that deliberate silence — is not weakness or hesitation. It is control. It tells the room: *I am not afraid of this moment. I own it.*

Speed may impress for a few seconds. Clarity convinces long after you leave the room.

Rajan, by the way, got a second interview. He prepared differently this time. Not new words. No more rehearsal. Just one instruction he gave himself before walking in: *breathe, and let the pauses do their work.*

He got the job

The Confidence Myth

There is a story about Malala Yousafzai that rarely gets told in the highlight reels.

In 2009, an eleven-year-old girl from Mingora — a small city in Pakistan's Swat Valley — agreed to give her first on-camera interview. The Taliban had banned girls from attending school and were tightening their grip on the region. Malala had been writing an anonymous blog for the BBC under a false name, Gul Makai, describing what life felt like under that control. But speaking on camera, with her real face and her real voice, was different. It was visible. It was dangerous.

PERSONALITY PROFILE

Malala Yousafzai

Born 1997 • Pakistan

Pakistani activist and the youngest Nobel Peace Prize laureate in history. At eleven, she gave her first on-camera interview calling for girls' right to education — afraid, but speaking anyway. Shot by the Taliban at fifteen, she recovered and continued with greater conviction than before.

COMMUNICATION LESSON

Malala did not wait to feel confident before speaking.
She spoke while afraid — and confidence arrived because she did.
Competence creates confidence. Not the other way around.

She was afraid. She has said this herself. In her memoir she describes the fear that lived with her constantly — not the absence of fear, but the decision to move forward despite it. In that first interview, her voice was young, uncertain in places, clearly the voice of a child who had not yet found the full weight of what she was carrying. She said simply: *"You must have the confidence to say that this thing is going wrong, and we must raise our voice."*

She did not feel the confidence she was describing. She was building it by speaking.

That eleven-year-old girl became the youngest Nobel Peace Prize laureate in history. The voice that addressed the United Nations at sixteen — measured, clear, completely without flinching — was not a different person from the frightened child who gave that first interview. It was the same person, with five more years of speaking despite the fear.

This is the truth that the Confidence Myth conveniently leaves out.

Most people are waiting. Waiting to feel ready. Waiting for the nervousness to disappear. Waiting for some internal signal that says now you are confident enough to begin. But that signal never comes — because confidence is not the starting point. It is the destination. And the only road that leads there is action.

Confidence is not a personality trait you are either born with or denied. It is a byproduct — something that gets produced when preparation meets repetition. When you know your structure, when you have practised your delivery, when you have stood in front of a mirror or a small audience enough times that the discomfort begins to shrink — that is when confidence quietly shows up.

Waiting to feel confident before speaking is like waiting to feel strong before going to the gym. Strength is built inside the gym. Confidence is built inside the conversation.

Competence creates confidence. Not the other way around.

The Personality Myth

At some point, someone probably told you — or you told yourself — that you are simply not the type.

"I'm an introvert. I'm not naturally expressive. Some people are just built for this and I'm not."

It is a comfortable story. It also happens to be wrong.

Communication is not a personality contest. It is not awarded to the loudest person in the room, the one who speaks the most or the one who commands attention through sheer energy. History has quietly but consistently proven this.

A.P.J. Abdul Kalam never performed. He never raised his voice to fill a room. He spoke slowly, in simple language, with the calm of someone who had nothing to prove. Yet entire auditoriums of thousands of students would go completely silent when he spoke. Not out of obligation — out of genuine attention. Because every word he said was clear. Every explanation was structured. He was not trying to sound impressive. He was trying to be understood.

That is the entire secret.

Loudness creates noise. Clarity creates impact. An extrovert who speaks without structure leaves people entertained but empty. An introvert who speaks with precision leaves people changed. Personality sets your natural volume. It does not determine your ability to communicate. Structure does. And structure is a skill. Skills can be learned.

The Real Definition

So if communication is not about fluency, speed, confidence, or personality — what is it actually about?

Here is the definition on which this entire book is built on:

Communication is the disciplined process of transferring clarity from your mind into someone else's mind.

Read that again slowly. The keyword is *transfer*. It is not enough that the idea exists clearly inside your head. It is not enough that you said the right words or used the right tone. The only question that matters is this: did the other person receive exactly what you intended to send?

If they did not — if they walked away confused, uncertain, or with a different understanding than you intended — then communication did not occur. A speech happened, perhaps. Words were exchanged. But the fundamental purpose was not fulfilled.

This single shift in definition changes everything. It moves the responsibility from *how you sound* to *how clearly you transfer*. It stops you from performing and starts you thinking about your listener — their context, their understanding, their ability to follow your thinking step by step.

Before you work on your voice, your vocabulary, your body language, or your storytelling, correct the definition you are working from.

Communication is not about sounding impressive.

It is about being understood.

Exercise : The Clarity Test

Before you read another word of this book, do this.

Take out your phone. Open the voice recorder. Press record — and explain, in your own words, your answer to this single question:

"What is communication?"

You have sixty seconds. No notes. No preparation. Just speak.

Then put your phone down and do not listen to it yet.

Come back after twenty-four hours. Find a quiet place, close any distractions, and press play. This time, you are not the speaker. You are the observer. Listen the way you would listen to a stranger — with honest, neutral attention.

As you listen, ask yourself five questions:

- Was my idea actually clear, or did it circle without landing?
- Did I rush through any part of it?
- Did I repeat the same point in different words without realising?
- Did I fill silences with *um*, *like*, *you know*, or *basically*?
- Did my sentences have a beginning, a middle, and an end — or did they just stop?

Do not judge what you hear emotionally. Do not cringe and switch it off. Simply observe. Note what you notice. That is all.

This exercise is not about performing well. It is about seeing yourself clearly — perhaps for the first time. Most people have never truly heard themselves speak. They have only felt themselves speak, which is an entirely different experience.

Awareness is where every improvement begins. Not motivation. Not talent. Not the right course or the perfect teacher.

Awareness.

This book will give you the tools. But the work begins the moment you are willing to listen to yourself honestly.

Turn the page when you are ready — not just to read, but to practise.

Chapter 2

Why Most People Quit — And How Skill Actually Forms

There is a moment that happens to almost every student who takes communication seriously.

It usually comes about a week in. They have done the exercises. They have recorded themselves. They have heard the gaps — the rushing, the filler words, the collapsed sentences. And they felt something rare and valuable: genuine awareness. For the first time, they could see exactly what needed to change.

So they begin. They slow down deliberately. They pause before answering. They breathe before speaking. They think about structure before opening their mouth.

And then something deeply uncomfortable happens.

They sound *worse.*

The pauses feel robotic. The breathing feels performed. The structure feels like scaffolding that hasn't been hidden yet — visible and clunky and completely unnatural. They listen back to a recording and think: *I sounded more confident before I started trying.*

And right there, in that exact moment of doubt, most people quietly put the book down, close the app, and walk away.

Not because they lacked the ability. Because they misread the signal.

The Discomfort Phase

What that student was experiencing was not failure. It was not regression. It had nothing to do with talent or potential or whether they were "built" for this.

What they were experiencing was skill formation. And skill formation, in its early stages, always feels like falling apart before it feels like coming together.

Think about the first time you learned to drive. You had done it mentally a hundred times — you had watched others do it your whole life, it looked effortless. Then you sat behind the wheel and suddenly had to think about the clutch, the mirrors, the steering, the distance, the gear, the brake — all simultaneously. You were slower and more dangerous than someone who had never thought about driving at all.

Were you failing? No. Your brain was running two systems at once: the old automatic one that had always been a passenger, and the new conscious one desperately trying to take the wheel. That internal collision creates friction. And friction feels like incompetence.

It is not incompetence. It is rewiring.

How the Brain Actually Builds Skill

Your brain is, above all else, an efficient machine.

Every time you repeat a behaviour, your brain begins building a shortcut — a neural pathway that makes that behaviour faster, smoother, and cheaper to run. This is why experienced drivers barely think about changing gears. This is why a trained musician's fingers find the notes before their mind has finished naming them. The behaviour has been repeated so many times that it no longer requires conscious energy.

Now think about your communication habits. If you have rushed through sentences for years, that pathway is deeply worn. If you have avoided structuring your thoughts before speaking, that shortcut is strong and fast. Your brain is very good at doing what it has always done.

So when you introduce a new behaviour — slowing down, pausing, breathing deliberately — your brain does not celebrate. It resists. Because new pathways are expensive. They require energy, attention, and effort. And the brain sends very convincing messages to talk you out of it:

This feels strange. This is too much effort. This isn't natural.

Here is the single most important thing to understand about those messages: **natural simply means familiar. It does not mean it is correct. And it does not mean it is effective.**

The goal is not to do what feels natural. The goal is to repeat the right thing until it becomes natural.

The Four Stages of Mastery

Every skill — without exception — travels through four predictable stages. Most people abandon the journey because no one told them what the map looks like.

Stage One: Unconscious Incompetence.

You do not know what you do not know. You rush, lose structure, use filler words — and feel completely fine about it, because you cannot yet see it. There is comfort here, but it is the comfort of unawareness.

Stage Two: Conscious Incompetence.

Awareness arrives — and with it, discomfort. You now notice your breath collapsing mid-sentence. You catch the *um* before it fades. You hear the moment your structure falls apart. You see the gap between where you are and where you want to be.

This is the most dangerous stage — not because it is the hardest, but because it *feels* like regression. You were more comfortable before you knew. And so the mind whispers: *you were better before you started trying.*

This is where most people quit.

But here is the truth that changes everything: you have not gotten worse. You have simply learned to *see.* And seeing clearly is the beginning of every transformation.

Stage Three: Conscious Competence.

You can do it — but only with effort. You slow down intentionally and it works. You structure your answer deliberately and the clarity shows. You control your breathing and your voice steadies. It is not automatic yet. It demands focus. But it is real. The skill exists now. It simply needs repetition to find its rhythm.

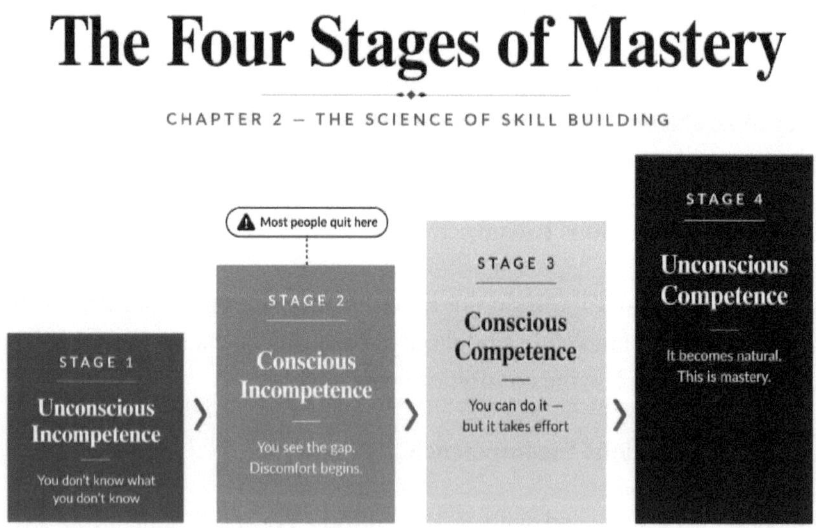

Discomfort at Stage 2 is not failure — it is your brain rewiring itself.

Stage Four: Unconscious Competence.

The skill disappears into the background — which is exactly where great skill belongs. You no longer remind yourself to pause. Structure activates before you consciously call for it. Your breathing supports your voice without instruction. What was once a deliberate act has become a natural expression.

And when someone watches you and says, *"You're such a natural communicator"* — you will know exactly what that means. Not gifted. Not lucky. **Trained.**

When I first became serious about improving my communication, progress felt surprisingly easy. I learned frameworks, studied body language, read books, watched lectures, and filled pages of my diary with communication principles and methods. The knowledge came quickly, and for a while it felt as though I was making rapid progress simply because I understood more than I had before.

Then I started applying what I had learned.

That is when everything began to feel wrong. Instead of speaking naturally, I found myself constantly monitoring my behaviour. I was thinking about my posture, my breathing, my pace, my structure, and my eye contact. Every conversation felt like a task rather than a conversation. Instead of feeling more confident, I felt less like myself. I remember wondering why I suddenly had to think before speaking. Why did every answer require conscious effort? Why did it feel as if I was playing the role of a communicator rather than simply being one?

Before learning these skills, I could speak without analysing every detail. Now I was analysing everything. Ironically, the more aware I became, the worse I felt. I genuinely believed my communication had deteriorated. Looking back, I can see that I had entered Stage Two, but at the time I had no language for what I was experiencing. I had developed awareness, but I had not yet developed automaticity.

The discomfort became so frustrating that I eventually stopped practising altogether. Not for a week. Not for a month. For nearly five months. The knowledge remained in my diary, the frameworks remained on paper, and the intentions remained in my mind, but the practice disappeared. I convinced myself that perhaps I was overcomplicating something that should have felt natural.

Then something unexpected happened.

I started creating podcasts. For the first time, I was not just participating in conversations; I was observing them. I listened carefully to my own recordings and to the way my guests communicated. I began noticing patterns, strengths, weaknesses, habits, and blind spots. I could hear moments where a guest lost structure, where a story became engaging, where a pause created impact, or where confidence disappeared. More importantly, I could hear the same patterns in myself.

That experience forced me to confront an important truth. The skills had never been the problem. The discomfort had been. I had mistaken the feeling of rewiring for the feeling of failure. What I interpreted as evidence that the methods were not working was actually evidence that they were working exactly as they should.

So I started again. This time I expected the awkwardness. I expected the frustration. I expected the feeling that nothing was becoming natural fast enough. Because I understood the process, I no longer interpreted discomfort as a signal to stop.

Today, I would place myself somewhere between Stage Three and Stage Four. Many of the skills that once required conscious effort now happen automatically. Structure appears more naturally, pauses feel intentional rather than forced, and awareness no longer fights against delivery. There is still room to improve, and there always will be, but the difference between then and now is that I understand what growth actually feels like.

If you are currently in Stage Two and questioning whether something is wrong with you, I want you to know that nothing is wrong. You are simply standing in the most uncomfortable stage of skill development. The mistake is not feeling awkward. The mistake is leaving before the awkwardness has time to become ability. The discomfort is not evidence that you are failing. It is evidence that change is happening.

Understanding Your Blind Spots — The Johari Window

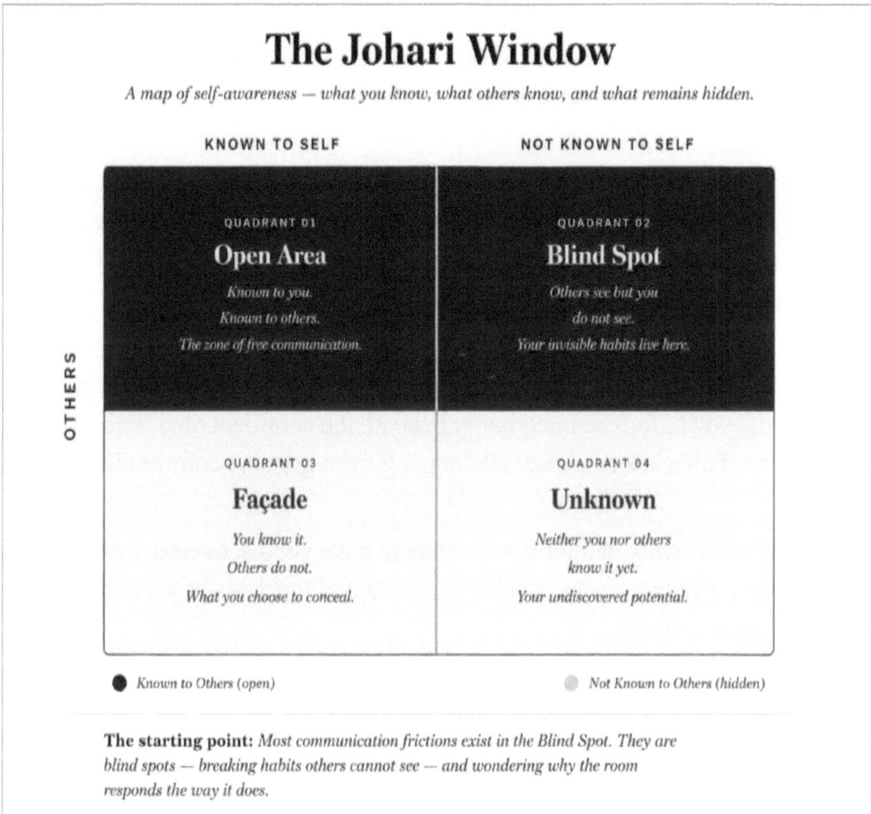

In 1955, two American psychologists — Joseph Luft and Harry Ingham — created a simple but deeply useful model for understanding self-awareness. They named it the Johari Window, combining their first names. It was designed to map the gap between how we see ourselves and how others experience us.

I came across this framework through a video by Destin Sandlin — an aerospace engineer who runs the YouTube channel Smarter Every Day. The video is titled What Everyone Sees... But I Don't, and it is exactly what that title promises — a genuinely honest exploration of what others observe in us that we are completely blind to ourselves.

The model divides awareness into four quadrants.

The Open Area is what you know about yourself and what others also know. This is the zone of free, confident communication. The larger this quadrant, the more effective your communication.

The Blind Spot is what others can clearly see in you that you cannot see in yourself. Your rushed pace. Your filler words. The way your posture collapses when you are uncertain. These habits are completely visible to your listener and completely invisible to you — until someone holds up a mirror.

The Façade is what you know about yourself but choose not to reveal. The nervousness you hide. The uncertainty beneath the confident tone. Energy spent maintaining the façade is energy taken away from genuine communication.

The Unknown is what neither you nor others have yet discovered about you — undeveloped strengths, untested abilities, potential that has not yet had the right environment to emerge.

Now here is why this matters for Stage Two specifically.

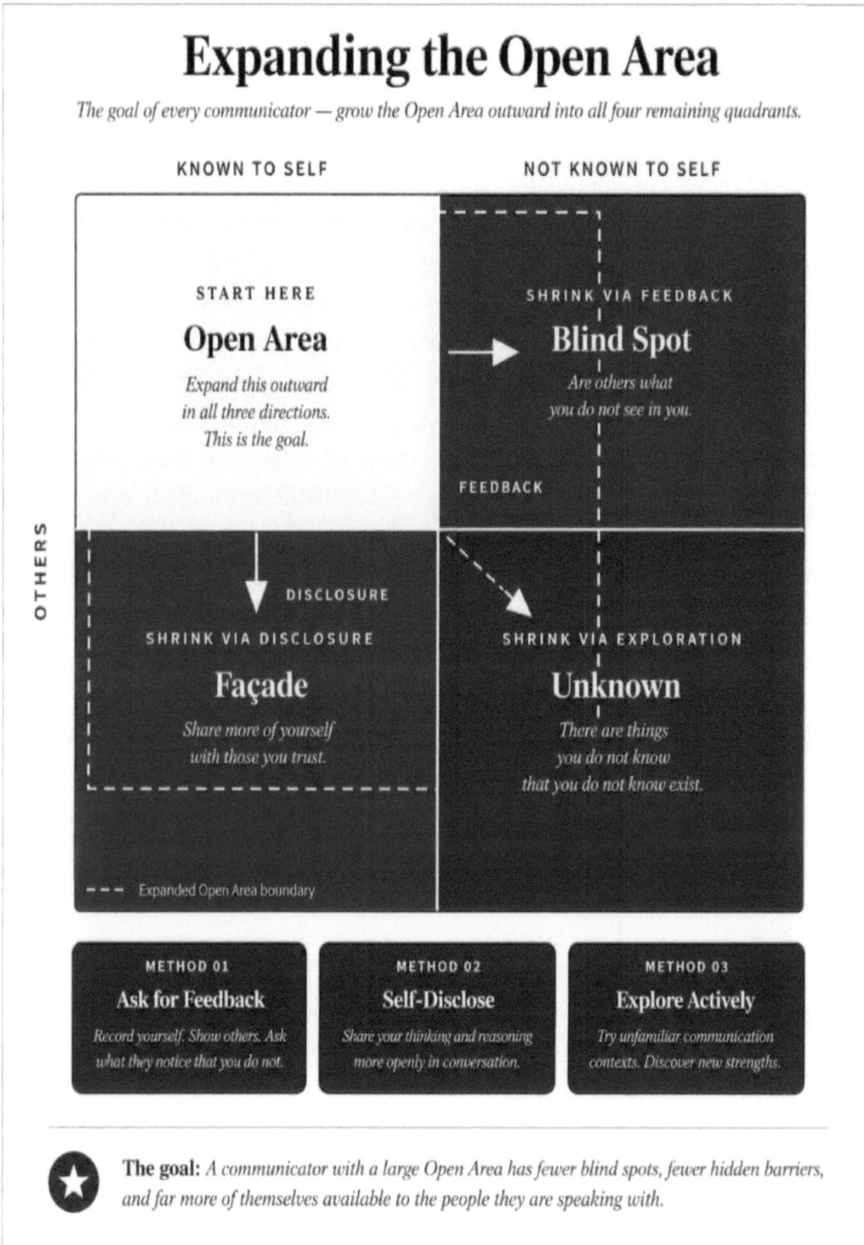

When you begin practising communication deliberately — when you first record yourself, first hear the gaps, first feel the discomfort of conscious correction — your Blind Spot is at its largest. You are becoming aware of things that were always there but never visible. That sudden visibility is not regression. It is the Blind Spot beginning to shrink.

The goal of every communicator is not to eliminate all four quadrants. It is to grow the Open Area — deliberately, consistently, in three specific directions. You shrink the Blind Spot through feedback. Record yourself. Ask trusted people what they notice. Read the room. Every piece of honest external observation moves something from your Blind Spot into your Open Area. You shrink the Façade through disclosure. Share your thinking more openly. Acknowledge uncertainty when it is real. Communicate what is actually happening rather than performing a version of what you think should be happening. Authenticity is not weakness — it is the fastest route to connection. You shrink the Unknown through exploration. Attempt communication contexts that feel unfamiliar. Speak in rooms that stretch you. The strengths you do not yet know you have only reveal themselves when you put yourself in situations that require them.

Every stage of mastery in this chapter maps directly onto the Johari Window. Stage One is a large Blind Spot with a small Open Area. Stage Four is a large Open Area with a Blind Spot that has been substantially reduced through years of feedback, practice, and honest self-observation. The discomfort of Stage Two is simply the Blind Spot getting smaller. And a shrinking Blind Spot is never a reason to stop.

The Real Reason People Quit

They quit in Stage Two. Every time.

They experience the discomfort of conscious correction and conclude that the method is broken, that the skill is beyond them, that they simply are not the type. They say *I sounded better before* — and they are half right. They sounded more *familiar than before*. More automatic. More like the old pattern they had been running for years.

But familiarity is not better. It is just known.

You cannot automate what you have not first consciously practised. The awkward stage is not optional. It is the process. Every person who now speaks with ease and structure and calm authority was once standing in that exact uncomfortable place, deciding whether the discomfort meant *stop* or *continue.*

The ones who continued are the ones you admire today.

The Rule of Repetition

Confidence is not created by reading about communication. It is not created by watching videos, attending seminars, or feeling inspired at midnight.

It is created by one thing: **repeated, structured action under slight discomfort.**

Every time you practise correctly, you strengthen a new pathway. Every time you return to the old habit, you reinforce the one you are trying to replace. This is not motivational language. It is biology. The brain responds to repetition — not intention.

If you repeat correctly and consistently, improvement is not just possible. It is inevitable.

Exercise : Identify Your Stage

Before turning to this page, stop and answer honestly.

Right now, in your communication, which stage are you in? Not where you want to be. Where you actually are.

- Are you in Stage One — comfortable but unaware?
- Are you in Stage Two — aware, uncomfortable, and tempted to quit?
- Are you in Stage Three — improving, but only with effort?
- Are you in Stage Four — or approaching it?

Write it down. Date it. Come back to this page in sixty days and read it again.

And from this moment forward, make one agreement with yourself: when practice feels awkward and forced and mechanical — do not interpret that as failure.

Interpret it as evidence that rewiring is happening.

The discomfort is not a wall. It is a doorway. And it only opens in one direction — forward.

Exercise 2B: Expand Your Open Area

The Johari Window suggests that communication improves when your Open Area grows. You do that by reducing your Blind Spot, your Façade, and your Unknown Area.Take five minutes and answer the questions below.

Blind Spot

What is one communication habit that other people may notice about you more clearly than you notice about yourself?

Façade

What is one thought, feeling, or opinion you often hold back during conversations

---

Unknown

What communication situation do you usually avoid because it makes you uncomfortable?

One Action

Choose one small action you will take this week to expand your Open Area.

Examples:

- Ask someone for honest feedback.
- Speak up once in a group discussion.
- Share an opinion you would normally keep to yourself.
- Volunteer to introduce yourself to someone new.

My action:

Remember: awareness is not created by confidence. It is created by observation. Every Blind Spot you discover, every mask you remove, and every challenge you face expands your Open Area and makes you a more effective communicator.

PART II

STRUCTURED THINKING

Most people try to fix communication at the surface — pronunciation, vocabulary, confidence tricks. These are not wrong, but they are the wrong place to start. It is like repainting the walls of a house whose foundation is cracked. The result holds for a moment. Then the cracks return. Because the root of almost every communication problem is not in the mouth. It is in the mind.

Clarity begins before you speak. When thinking is scattered, sentences scatter. When ideas have no order, speech has no direction. But when thinking becomes structured — organized, sequenced, purposeful — speech does not just improve. It transforms. You did not need more words. You needed to know where to put them.

CAN YOU UNTANGLE
YOUR MIND?

CHAPTER 3

Fix Your Thinking Before You Fix Your Voice

There is a particular kind of frustration that intelligent people know well.

You are in a conversation — an interview, a discussion, a presentation — and you *know* the answer. The information is there. You have read about it, thought about it, lived it perhaps. But the moment you open your mouth, something goes wrong. The words arrive in the wrong order. One idea pulls you toward another before the first one is finished. You find yourself circling back, repeating, filling the gaps with *um* and *basically* and *you know* — and somewhere in the middle of your own sentence, you lose the thread entirely.

You walk away thinking: *My English failed me. My confidence failed me.*

But neither of those is what actually happened.

Your *thinking* failed you. And that is a completely different problem — with a completely different solution.

Why Rambling Happens

When someone asks you a question, your brain is not doing one thing. It is doing three things simultaneously: retrieving information, organising that information, and converting it into spoken language — all in real time, all under social pressure.

When you have no internal structure prepared, the brain improvises. And improvisation under pressure is expensive. The mental energy that should be going toward *delivery* gets consumed by *searching*. The result is what every speaker dreads — long pauses, repeated phrases, incomplete ideas, and a trail of filler words that appear not because your vocabulary is poor, but because your brain is buying itself time to find direction.

This is not a language problem. It is a cognitive load problem. And the solution is not more vocabulary. It is less chaos — which means more structure.

When you know the shape of your response before you begin speaking, something remarkable happens. The retrieval, organising, and delivery no longer compete for the same mental resource. Delivery becomes calmer. Clarity increases. And confidence — that elusive quality everyone wants but few know how to build — arrives naturally as a consequence.

Your Primary Thinking Backbone

From this point forward, you have a default structure for almost any response you will ever need to give:

Problem → Cause → Solution

Three parts. Always in that order. Memorise it the way you memorised your address.

This structure works because it mirrors the way the human mind naturally seeks to understand the world. When you open with a problem, you create attention — the listener leans in because something needs resolving. When you explain the cause, you create understanding — the *why* behind the *what*. When you offer a solution, you create closure — and the mind relaxes because the loop has been closed.

Without closure, conversations feel unfinished. You have probably experienced this — sitting through an answer that went on and on and somehow never actually arrived anywhere. That is a speech without a destination. Problem → Cause → Solution gives your words a destination before you even begin.

Let's make it concrete.

Question: Why do students struggle with communication?

Unstructured answer: *"I think it's because, like, students don't really practise enough, and also maybe they're nervous, and the vocabulary is also sometimes a problem, and teachers don't always help either..."*

Structured answer: *"The core problem is that most students try to improve communication at the surface — pronunciation, vocabulary, confidence — without addressing the root. The cause is a lack of structured thinking. When the mind has no framework, speech becomes scattered regardless of how much someone knows. The solution is to train thinking first. Once ideas have order, words follow naturally."*

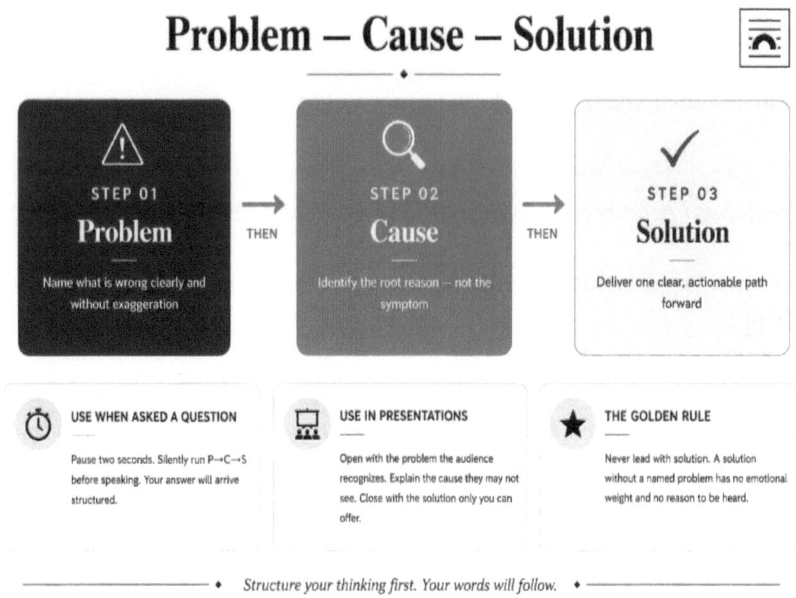

Same knowledge. Completely different impact. The second answer does not just sound more confident — it *is* more structured, and structure is what confidence sounds like from the outside.

How This Framework Opened Doors For Me

I want to tell you how I use this exact structure every time I approach a new school or institution with my communication masterclass — because the story will show you something about this framework that no example can.

The setting is always the same. A principal's office. A busy educator sitting across from a young person they have never met, with fifteen other things demanding their attention and no particular reason to listen. I have about three minutes before their attention moves elsewhere. Maybe less.

The first time I walked into a principal's office to pitch my masterclass, I had no reputation, no institutional backing, and no guarantee that anyone in that room had ever thought about communication skills as something worth dedicated time in a school schedule. What I had was the framework you just read.

I would sit down, thank them for the time, and begin.

"Sir, I want to share something I have been observing across classrooms — a problem that I believe is affecting students' futures more than their marks are."

That one sentence creates attention. The principal looks up. Something needs resolving.

"The problem is this —students are academically capable. They study hard, they prepare, they know their subjects. But when they enter a group discussion, face a job interview, stand up to present, or walk into a room where they need to represent themselves — they go silent. Not because they lack knowledge. Because they were never taught how to communicate what they know."

Now the listener is nodding. They have seen this. Every educator in every school has watched a capable student freeze in a situation that required them to speak rather than write.

"The cause is simple. Our curriculum builds knowledge but it does not build expression. From Class 1 to graduation, students are trained to absorb information and reproduce it on paper. They are almost never trained to think on their feet, structure their ideas under pressure, or command a room with their presence. The skill gap is not in their intelligence. It is in the one area no syllabus currently covers."

By this point in the conversation, the principal is no longer passively listening. They are thinking about specific students. Specific situations they have witnessed. The problem has become personal.

"The solution I am proposing is a structured communication masterclass — a programme that builds this skill from the ground up, using practical exercises, real frameworks, and the kind of repetition that actually changes behaviour rather than just informing it. This book" — and here I place a copy on the table — *"is the companion to that programme. Every student who attends the session leaves with a resource they can return to."*

Three parts. Problem. Cause. Solution. Delivered in the order the human mind needs them.

I have walked into principal offices where I was given three minutes and stayed for forty-five. Not because I am a particularly remarkable salesperson. Because the structure did the work. It gave the conversation a destination. And when a conversation has a clear destination, the listener does not experience it as a pitch. They experience it as a solution arriving at exactly the right moment.

That is what this framework does in the real world. It does not just organise your words. It organises the other person's thinking — and a person whose thinking you have organised is already halfway to agreeing with you.

The Two-Second Rule

In 1993, a young manager named Howard was being interviewed for a senior position at a consulting firm. The interviewer asked him a sharp, unexpected question: *"What is the biggest communication failure you have witnessed in a professional setting?"*

Howard's instinct was to start speaking immediately — to fill the silence before it became uncomfortable. Instead, he did something his mentor had once told him: he paused, took a breath, and silently asked himself three questions.

What is the problem here? What caused it? What is the solution?

Two seconds. Then he spoke.

"In my previous role, our project team missed a critical deadline — not because the work wasn't done, but because no one had communicated the delay clearly to the client. That is the problem. The cause was that each team member assumed someone else had already informed them. There was knowledge, but no ownership of communication. The solution we implemented was a single weekly update — one person, one message, one clear status. After that, we never had a miscommunication with that client again."

The interviewer stopped writing mid-note, looked up, and said: *"That is the most organised answer I have heard all week."*

Howard got the job. But more importantly, he never forgot what those two seconds taught him: that the pause is not weakness. The pause is the structure loading.

Before answering any important question, give yourself two seconds. Not to perform thinking — to actually do it. Ask yourself the three questions silently. Then speak.

Those two seconds will save you thirty seconds of rambling. Every time.

Exercise : The Structured Speaking Drill

Take these three questions. Answer each one out loud using Problem → Cause → Solution. Record yourself on your phone.

1. Why do people fear public speaking?
2. Why is communication important for career growth?
3. Why do students use filler words?

When you listen back, ask yourself three things: Did I follow the structure or drift away from it? Did I conclude clearly or trail off? Where did I lose direction — and why?

Do this for five minutes every day for one week. You are not trying to sound perfect. You are training your brain to reach for structure automatically — the way a driver reaches for the gear without looking down.

Structure becomes instinct through repetition. And once it becomes instinct, clarity stops being something you work at.

It becomes simply the way you think.

Chapter 4

Frameworks for Instant Clarity

In 1986, NASA launched the space shuttle Challenger into a cold Florida morning. Within seventy-three seconds, it broke apart. Seven astronauts were lost.

What the world remembers as an engineering failure was also, at its core, a communication failure.

The engineers who understood the risk were not silent. They had data. They had concerns. They had raised the issue of O-ring seals performing dangerously in low temperatures the night before the launch. The information existed. The warning existed. The doubt existed.

But the message never landed with enough clarity, structure, or conviction to stop the decision.

Numbers were presented without context. Concerns were voiced without a clear recommendation. The people in the room who needed to act did not feel the weight of what was being communicated. And so the launch proceeded.

This is not a story about villains. It is a story about what happens when critical information is not delivered with structure. The engineers knew. But knowing is not communicating. Clarity is communicating. And that night, clarity was absent — with irreversible consequences.

Most communication failures, of course, are quieter than this. Nothing explodes. No headline is written. A student knows the correct answer but explains it poorly and loses marks. A candidate prepares for months but drifts during an interview and loses the opportunity. A professional has a genuinely strong idea but presents it without structure and watches someone else get the credit.

The opportunity simply moves on. Silently.

As we discussed in the previous chapter, unstructured thinking is the root of unclear speech. You now have your foundational tool — Problem → Cause → Solution — for organising thoughts internally before you speak. That framework works on the inside.

This chapter gives you tools for the outside. Frameworks that help you *deliver* ideas clearly, completely, and with authority — especially when the pressure is high and the stakes are real.

The PARA Framework

When NASA's engineers presented their concerns, what they lacked was not data — it was a delivery structure that forced completeness. They had a point. They did not have a clear action, a stated result, or a definitive ask. The loop was never closed.

PARA closes the loop.

P — Point. State your core idea immediately. No background, no context-setting, no warming up. The listener should know within your first sentence what this is about.

A — Action. What specifically happened or what specifically you did. Not how you felt — what you *did.*

R — Result. What changed as a measurable or observable outcome.

A — Ask. Where does this go next? What do you want, propose, or recommend?

Let's apply it to the most common high-pressure communication moment most people face.

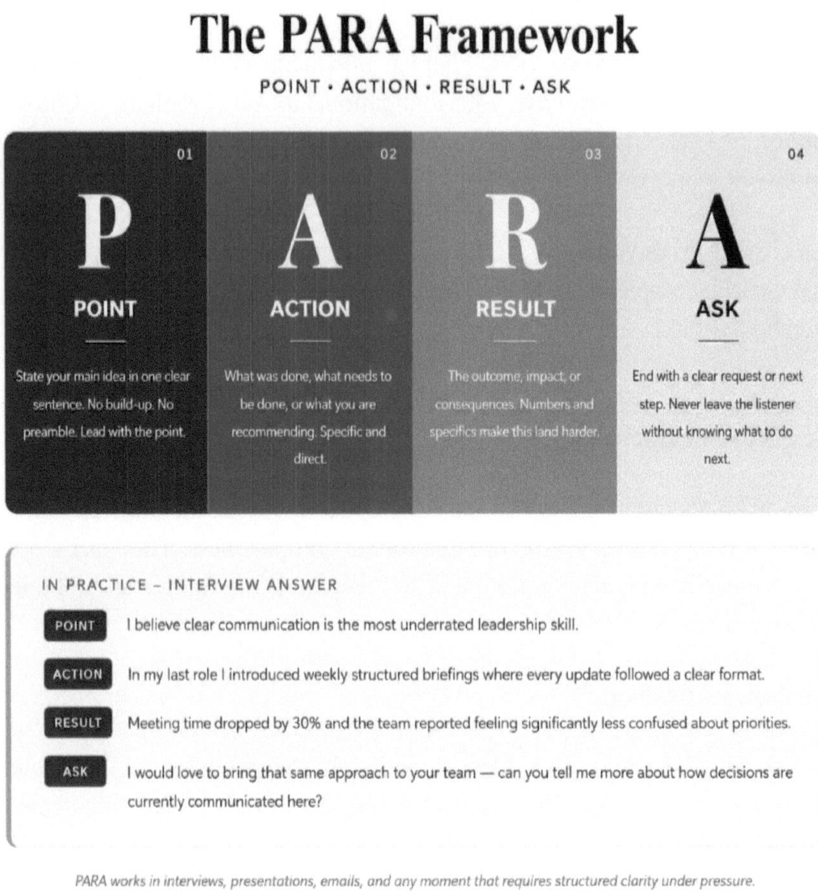

Interview Question: *"Tell me about a challenge you handled."*

Unstructured answer: *"We had some issues in the team and I tried to help and it was quite difficult but we managed somehow in the end..."*

Structured using PARA:

"Our project team was missing deadlines because responsibilities weren't clearly assigned — that was the core problem (**Point***) . I mapped out every task, assigned individual ownership, and introduced a brief weekly check-in to*

catch blocks early (**Action***). Within three weeks, our delivery time improved and the back-and-forth confusion dropped significantly (***Result***). Going forward, I intend to apply this same approach wherever I work — because I've seen firsthand what structured coordination does for a team."(* **Ask***)*

Notice what PARA does. It does not just make the answer longer or more impressive. It makes it *complete.* The listener does not have to wonder what happened, what you did, or what you are proposing. Every question is answered before it is asked.

Incomplete answers create doubt. Complete answers create trust.

The 3-2-1 Method

Not every situation gives you time to build a full structured response. Sometimes a question arrives without warning. Sometimes a conversation shifts direction mid-sentence. Sometimes you have thirty seconds and no preparation. This is where 3-2-1 becomes your fastest tool.

The method is simple: before you begin speaking, decide on one number — and anchor your answer to it. That number becomes a mental track that keeps your response from drifting into scattered territory.

One important clarification before you read further. The method is not called 3-2-1 because you use all three numbers together. It is called 3-2-1 because those are your three options — and you choose only one depending on what the moment requires. A complex topic with multiple dimensions might call for three points. A direct comparison needs two. A single defining idea needs only one. The skill is in choosing the right number before you open your mouth — not in using all of them at once.

Here is what each option looks like in practice.

Imagine someone asks you without warning — *what do you think about communication skills?* You have three seconds. You pick a number and begin.

Using 3: "Communication matters for three reasons — academic clarity, career growth, and stronger relationships."
Using 2: "It impacts two major areas — professional success and personal influence."
Using 1: "The single most important reason communication matters is that it shapes how people perceive your intelligence — fairly or not."
Now notice something. The topic was communication — something directly connected to this book and easy to pull examples from. But the 3-2-1 method works on anything. Completely random topics. Unprepared moments. Subjects you have never formally studied.

Try this one. Someone at a dinner table turns to you and asks — *what do you think makes a good film?*
You have not prepared. You have no notes. You pick a number and begin.
Using 3: "I think three things make a great film — a story that feels real, at least one character you genuinely care about, and an ending that stays with you after you leave the theatre."
Using 2: "For me it comes down to two things — direction and performance. You can have a weak script and still make something powerful if both of those are right."
Using 1: "The single thing that separates a good film from a great one is whether it makes you feel something you were not expecting to feel."
None of those answers required preparation. None required expertise in cinema. They required only a number — chosen in the two seconds before speaking — and the discipline to build the answer inside that structure rather than outside it. That is the method working exactly as it should. On any topic. In any room. With zero warning.
The number does something specific to the brain — both yours and your listener's. For you, it creates a committed structure before you start. If you say three, your brain immediately begins searching for three things rather than broadcasting everything at once. If you say one, your brain is forced to identify what actually matters most rather than listing everything it can find. For your listener, the number creates an expectation — they know what shape the answer

will take before it arrives, so they listen with a framework instead of passively waiting for you to finish.
Think of it as giving your listener a container before you pour.

A student once told me she used to panic the moment a professor called on her unexpectedly. Her mind would go blank and her first instinct was to apologise — "Sorry, I'm not sure" — before she had even tried. She started practising 3-2-1 daily on random topics for two minutes each morning. The rule was simple: pick a topic, choose a number, speak. Within three weeks her default response to any unexpected question had become — "I think there are two key reasons for this" — and by the time she said it her brain had already found the two reasons. The structure arrived before the content and pulled the content in behind it.
That is what the right number does. It does not just tell the listener how many points are coming. It tells your own brain how many to find — and the brain, given a specific target, almost always delivers.

The Pyramid Principle — Lead With the Answer

Most people, when asked to explain something or present an idea, begin at the beginning. They provide the background first, then the context, then the details, and finally — after the listener has been waiting through all of it — they arrive at the point.

This is the natural sequence of thinking. You work through the problem chronologically, and then you present it the same way you experienced it. The problem is that the listener did not experience the problem with you. They are arriving fresh, and what they need first is not your journey — it is your conclusion.

The Pyramid Principle, developed by Barbara Minto while working at McKinsey and Company, reverses this entirely. The structure is simple: lead with your answer, then support it.

It works like this. State your conclusion or recommendation first, clearly and without preamble. Then provide the two or three strongest supporting arguments. Then add the evidence or detail beneath each argument only if the listener needs it.

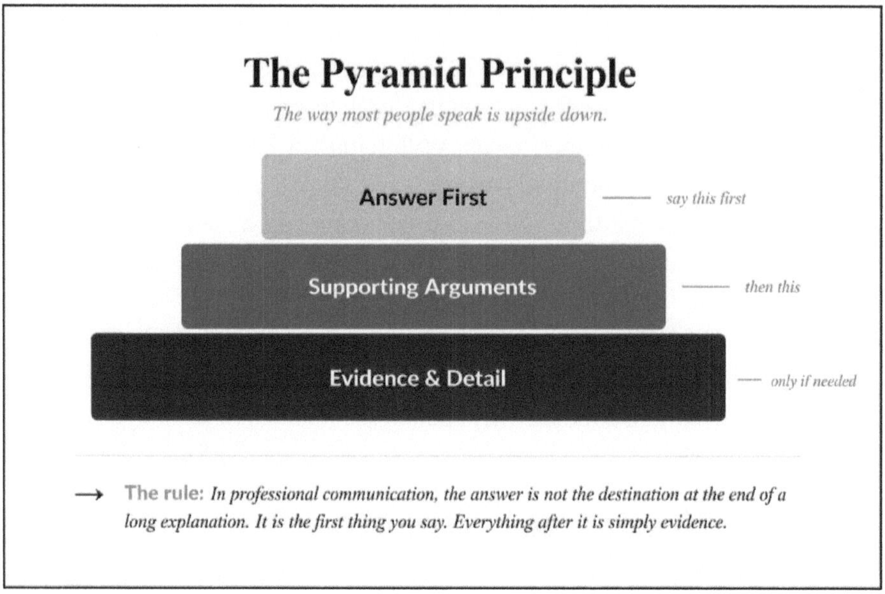

Consider the difference between these two approaches — and this time, forget the boardroom. Imagine you are trying to convince your closest friend to watch a film with you tonight.

First approach: "So basically I was scrolling through my phone and I saw this recommendation and I thought it looked interesting so I watched like the first twenty minutes and the cinematography was actually really different from what I expected and there is this one scene early on that kind of sets up the whole dynamic and I think the lead actor does something in that scene that most actors would not have done and also the soundtrack is apparently composed by someone who worked on a film we both really liked and I just think overall it might be something we would both enjoy and maybe we should watch it together sometime if you want."

Second approach: "You need to watch this film with me tonight. It is the best thing I have seen in six months. The lead actor does something in the first scene that will make you forget you are watching a film. The soundtrack is by the same composer as *Interstellar*. And the ending will genuinely stay with you for days. I am not watching it without you."

Same information. Completely different experience of receiving it.

The first approach makes the listener work. They are processing detail without knowing where it is going or why it matters. Their attention drifts because there is no destination in sight. The second approach tells them immediately what you are recommending — *watch this with me tonight* — and then gives them three sharp reasons to say yes. Their attention is directed from the first sentence rather than scattered across the explanation.

Notice also what the second approach does emotionally. It creates excitement before the evidence arrives. The conclusion — *you need to watch this with me tonight* — is not just information. It is an invitation with energy behind it. When you lead with your answer, you are not just organising your communication. You are giving the listener a reason to lean in before you have even begun to explain.

That is the Pyramid Principle working at its best. Not a corporate tool. A human one. Applicable to any conversation where you want someone to receive your thinking with the attention it deserves — whether you are in a boardroom, a classroom, or a conversation with someone you care about.

Exercise — Pyramid Reversal

Take any explanation or update you have given recently — in a meeting, in an email, in a conversation. Write it out the way you actually delivered it. Then rewrite it using the Pyramid Principle. Lead with the conclusion. Add three supporting points. Add evidence beneath each only if necessary. Compare the two versions and notice which one a busy professional would rather receive.

Frameworks Don't Make You Robotic. They Make You Reliable.

There is a concern some people raise when they first encounter communication frameworks: *won't this make me sound scripted? Won't people notice the structure?*

Consider this. When you watch a skilled architect present a building design, you do not think — *"this person is using a structured presentation."* You think — *"this person clearly knows what they are talking about."* The structure is invisible. What is visible is confidence, clarity, and authority.

That is what these frameworks do when practised enough. They disappear into the background, leaving only the impression of someone who thinks clearly and speaks with purpose.

Without structure, speech is reactive — it responds to whatever the brain retrieves first. With structure, speech is intentional — it moves toward a destination. And intentional speech, as we will continue to see throughout this book, is what earns credibility.

Credibility determines who gets heard. In a room full of equally intelligent people, the one who communicates with the most clarity will always carry the most influence.

Exercise : Real-World Application

Using PARA, answer the following out loud and record yourself:

1. Describe a time you faced a challenge and how you handled it.
2. Explain a failure and what you learned from it.
3. Suggest one improvement for your school or workplace.

Using 3-2-1, answer the following:

1. Why do students procrastinate?
2. What makes a good leader?
3. Why is discipline important?

When you listen back, ask yourself: Did I state my point immediately or did I circle into it? Did I conclude or did I trail off? Where did the structure hold — and where did it slip?

You are not aiming for perfection. You are training the brain to reach for a framework automatically — the way Howard reached for Problem → Cause → Solution in that interview room before a single word left his mouth.

Structure under pressure is not a gift. It is a habit. And habits form exactly the way we discussed in Chapter 2 — through conscious repetition until the effort disappears.

Exercise: The Random Word Drill

One of the biggest challenges in communication is not speaking when you are prepared—it is speaking when you are not. In interviews, discussions, presentations, and everyday conversations, you will often be asked questions you did not anticipate. Confidence in those moments comes from your ability to organise thoughts in real time.

To practise this skill, visit a website such as **randomwordgenerator.com** and generate a single random word. As soon as the word appears, put your phone down and speak about it for two to three minutes without preparation. Do not search for information, and do not restart if you get stuck.

If your mind goes blank, ask yourself: What is it? Where have I seen it? Why does it matter? What problem does it solve? What story or lesson is connected to it? These questions will help you generate ideas and maintain flow.

Whenever possible, record yourself and review the recording. Pay attention to filler words, long pauses, repetitive ideas, and weak structure. Over time, this exercise will improve your ability to think clearly, organise ideas quickly, and speak confidently under pressure.

The goal is not to become an expert on random topics. The goal is to become comfortable thinking while speaking.

In Part III, we move from how you think to how your body responds. Because even with perfect structure in your mind, fear has a way of arriving uninvited — and it arrives through your physiology first. The next chapter explains exactly what happens in your body when nervousness strikes, and more importantly, what to do about it.

PART III

PHYSIOLOGY & FEAR

By now, you understand structure. You know how to organize thoughts. But there is a moment every speaker experiences — a moment when the mind is ready, yet the body refuses to cooperate. Your heartbeat increases, your throat tightens, your breath becomes shallow, and your voice loses steadiness. At that moment, many people conclude that they are "not good at speaking."

That conclusion is inaccurate.

Communication is not only cognitive; it is physiological. When the body shifts into a stress response, delivery collapses — even if thinking remains clear. Before you improve your voice, you must understand what fear does to it. Because you cannot correct what you do not understand.

WHAT KEEPS YOU
PARALYZED?

CHAPTER 5

The Biology of Nervousness

Imagine you have prepared for weeks.

You know the material. You have practised the structure. You have rehearsed the opening three times in the mirror that morning. You walk into the room feeling ready — and then someone says *"you're up"* — and something happens that no amount of preparation seemed to prevent.

Your heart accelerates. Your throat tightens as though someone turned a dial. Your mouth goes dry. Your thoughts, which were perfectly ordered thirty seconds ago, begin to scatter. Your pace picks up without your permission. Your voice arrives thinner than it left your chest.

And then, five minutes after you sit down, the perfect sentence returns. Clear, calm, exactly right. Too late.

You walk away thinking you failed because your English wasn't strong enough, or your confidence wasn't there, or you simply aren't built for this.

But none of those things caused what happened.

Biology did.

What Your Brain Actually Does

When you stand up to speak in front of others, your brain does something it was designed to do for a very different situation. Deep inside the brain sits a small, almond-shaped structure called the amygdala. Its job is ancient and simple: scan for threats, and prepare the body to survive it.

The problem is that the amygdala cannot read context. It does not know the difference between a tiger emerging from the forest and thirty people watching you speak. Both register as exposure. Both trigger the same response. The moment it detects evaluation, uncertainty, or social risk — it fires.

Adrenaline floods the bloodstream. The heart accelerates to push blood toward large muscles. Breathing shortens to quicken oxygen delivery. The jaw and throat tighten. Fine motor control — the kind required for clear articulation — decreases. The brain narrows its focus to immediate survival rather than organised thought.

Every single one of these changes is useful if you need to run or fight.

Every single one of them is destructive if you need to speak.

Speech requires steady breath, relaxed muscles around the jaw and throat, and structured thinking moving in sequence. Adrenaline systematically disrupts all three. That is not a personal weakness. That is not a language gap. That is your nervous system doing exactly what it was built to do — in the wrong situation.

The Fear Loop

Here is where it becomes self-reinforcing.

Fear triggers adrenaline. Adrenaline shortens the breath. Shortened breath weakens vocal stability. An unstable voice increases self-consciousness. Self-consciousness amplifies fear. And fear triggers more adrenaline.

The loop tightens with every second you stand there trying to *think* your way out of a *physical* response.

This is why telling yourself to *calm down* or *be confident* almost never works in the moment. You are using language to address chemistry. It is the wrong tool for the problem.

If nervousness is biological, the solution must also be biological.

I want to tell you something I have never written down before.

When I was in Class 8, I transferred to a new school. A better school — more competitive, more structured, higher expectations. It should have been an opportunity. For me, at that age, it felt like a sentence.

This school had a culture of putting students on stage. Morning assembly, prayer recitation, public activities, announcements — students were expected to participate regularly and visibly. For students who had grown up in that environment, it was normal. For a new student arriving from a different background, with English that felt uncertain and a voice that felt unreliable, that stage was the most terrifying piece of architecture I had ever seen.

I developed a strategy. Not a good one.

I started arriving late deliberately — after the morning assembly had ended, after the stage had been cleared, after the moment where I might be called had safely passed. Every morning I calculated the exact window. Arrive too early and I risked being put on stage. Arrive at the right moment and I would slip into the classroom unnoticed.

It worked, in the way that avoidance always works — temporarily and at a cost. The cost was punishment. Regular, documented, increasingly serious punishment for repeated late arrival. I accepted it. The punishment felt manageable. The stage did not.

I told myself it was my English. That was the story I repeated every time the fear arrived — your English is not good enough, fix the English and the fear will go. So I did what that story demanded. I completed an entire Oxford English translation workbook. Every exercise. Every page. I worked through it with the kind of focus I had never applied to anything before.

My English improved. The fear did not move.

In an entire year at that school I stood on the stage twice to recite the prayer. Twice. And three or four times for compulsory activities where refusal was impossible. Every other appearance I avoided, deflected, or arrived too late to face.

In Class 9 I transferred again — this time to a Hindi medium school, for reasons unrelated to the stage. And something shifted. In Hindi I was confident. In Hindi I was among the top students. In Hindi the words came easily and the structure followed naturally and the voice that had felt so unreliable in English suddenly had weight behind it. Over two years I rebuilt something — not a technique, not a method, but a small, quiet belief that I was capable of being heard.

The proof came after my Class 10 results. My teachers organised a small celebration. Someone handed me a microphone in front of approximately two hundred people — students, teachers, parents — and I spoke for four minutes. Not perfectly. Not without a racing heart. But I spoke. Four minutes without stopping, without running, without arriving late to avoid it.

It had taken me three years.

Three years of the long way around — avoidance, punishment, transferring schools, rebuilding confidence slowly in a different language — to reach the place that the next section of this chapter will take you in a fraction of that time. I am not telling you this story to be inspiring. I am telling it because I need you to understand something that I did not understand at fourteen.

The fear I felt on that stage was not caused by my English. It was not caused by weakness or a lack of courage or any personal failing. It was caused by biology — a nervous system doing exactly what nervous systems are designed to do. I was experiencing the fear loop you just read about, with no knowledge of what it was and no tools to interrupt it.

You have something I did not have. You have the next section.

You do not need three years. Read on.

The Regulation Principle

Consider what actually happens in the body during an adrenaline response. Chemistry is preparing you for *movement* — for running, for physical effort, for exertion. When you stand still at a podium while adrenaline circulates, that energy has nowhere to go. It becomes trapped. And trapped activation appears as shaking hands, a trembling voice, a tight jaw, and thoughts that race without direction.

The solution is not suppression. It is *discharged.*

You need to give the adrenaline what it came for — movement — before you speak. This is not a motivational trick. It is nervous system management. And it works with a reliability that "trying to feel confident" never will.

Four Ways to Regulate Before You Speak

A brisk three-to-five minute walk is the simplest and most underrated tool available to any speaker. Walking allows the body to complete the movement response that adrenaline prepares. Heart rate rises briefly, circulation improves, breathing deepens naturally. When you stop, the nervous system transitions from panic activation into controlled readiness — alert, focused, calm. If you have a presentation, an interview, or an important conversation ahead, do not sit in a waiting room scrolling your phone. Walk.

Twenty star jumps serve a different purpose — speed. When you have two minutes and no corridor to walk down, a short burst of explosive movement rapidly burns through circulating adrenaline and increases oxygen intake. It feels slightly ridiculous. It works remarkably well. After thirty seconds of movement, breathing becomes deeper and more rhythmic, and vocal stability returns.

Five to ten push-ups work through grounding. The pressure through the arms and chest redirects anxious energy into controlled physical exertion. There is something about the deliberateness of the movement — the focus required — that pulls the mind out of the spiral and into the body. Two slow breaths after the last one, and you are ready.

Wim Hof Breathing — The Iceman's Method

In 1999, a Dutch man named Wim Hof stood submerged in ice water for one hour and fifty-two minutes. Scientists who studied him expected to find signs of hypothermia within minutes. Instead, they found something that contradicted everything they believed about the limits of human physiology. His core body temperature had barely moved. His nervous system was not in panic. It was regulated — deliberately, consciously, through breath.

Wim Hof, known worldwide as *The Iceman*, went on to climb Mount Everest in nothing but shorts and shoes, run a half marathon barefoot above the Arctic Circle, and set over twenty world records related to cold endurance. He has been studied by universities across Europe and the United States. What researchers consistently found was that his abilities were not the result of a rare genetic gift. They were the result of a specific, trainable breathing protocol that gave him conscious access to his own autonomic nervous system — the system that governs stress, fear, and physical regulation.

You do not need to sit in ice water. But the breathing component of his method is one of the most effective tools available for managing the adrenaline response before high-pressure communication. Used correctly and consistently, it creates a level of pre-performance calm that no motivational technique can replicate.

Here is how to do it properly.

Before You Begin

Find a quiet place where you can sit or lie down comfortably. Your spine should be supported. Your body should be relaxed — not rigid. This practice works best in the morning before an important day, or ten to fifteen minutes before a high-pressure speaking situation.

Important safety note: never practise this while driving, standing, near water, or in any situation where losing consciousness — however briefly — could cause harm. Light-headedness is normal. Fainting, though rare, is possible in early practice. Always be seated or lying down

The Practice — Step by Step

Round One

Begin breathing in deeply through your nose or mouth — whichever feels more natural. Fill your lungs completely. Feel your chest rise, then your belly expand. This is a full breath, not a half breath.

Now released. Do not force the exhale. Simply let it go — passively, without pushing. The exhale should feel like a release, not an effort.

Repeat this cycle thirty times. Keep a steady, rhythmic pace — roughly one full breath every three to four seconds. As you continue, you may begin to feel tingling in your fingers, your lips, or around your face. You may feel slightly lightheaded. This is normal. It is the result of shifting oxygen and carbon dioxide levels in your blood. Stay calm and continue breathing.

After your thirtieth breath, exhale completely — push every last bit of air out — and then *stop*. Do not inhale. Simply hold. Remain still and observe what you feel. You will likely feel a deep, quiet calm spreading through your body. Hold this empty breath for as long as feels comfortable — this typically ranges from thirty seconds to two minutes depending on your experience. Do not strain or compete with yourself. The moment you feel a genuine, natural urge to breathe — not panic, but a calm signal — that is your cue.

Recovery Breath

When that urge arrives, inhale one slow, deep breath — the deepest breath you can take. Fill your lungs completely and hold it for fifteen seconds. Feel your chest expand and your body stabilize. Then release slowly and naturally.

That completes Round One.

Round Two and Three

Rest for thirty to sixty seconds — breathing normally, quietly. Notice how your body feels. Most people report a noticeable shift after the first round: a quieting of internal noise, a steadiness in the chest, a sense of being more present than they were sixty seconds ago.

Then repeat the process — thirty deep breaths, empty breath hold, recovery breath — for a second and third round.

By the end of three rounds, something measurable has happened. The shallow, rapid breathing that stress produces — the kind that signals danger to the brain and keeps the fear loop running — has been interrupted and replaced. Oxygen levels have increased. Carbon dioxide tolerance has improved. And most importantly, your nervous system has received a clear biological signal: *the threat has passed. You are safe. You are ready.*

Why This Works for Speaking Specifically

Stress breathing is shallow. It lives in the upper chest and never fully reaches the lower lungs where the majority of oxygen exchange actually occurs. When you breathe shallowly for an extended period — as most people do when nervous — your brain interprets it as ongoing danger and continues releasing stress hormones. The fear loop has a physical fuel source, and shallow breathing is it.

Wim Hof breathing cuts off that fuel.

The deep breathing cycles flood the body with oxygen and create a temporary shift in blood chemistry that overrides the stress response. The breath retention phase does something additional and particularly valuable for speakers: it builds tolerance to internal physical discomfort. The racing heart, the tightness in the chest, the heightened physical awareness that comes with adrenaline — these sensations are often what push anxiety from manageable to overwhelming. When you train yourself to sit calmly inside those sensations during breath holds, you are rehearsing composure under pressure at a physiological level. The body learns that discomfort is not danger.

And when your body knows that — truly knows it — you can walk into a room of a hundred people, feel your heart rate rise, and think: *I know what this is. I know what to do with it.*

Practical Application

Use this method the morning of any high-stakes speaking situation — an interview, a presentation, a difficult conversation. Three full rounds takes approximately ten to fifteen minutes. The effect typically lasts two to three hours.

If you are unfamiliar with the technique, watch Wim Hof's official guided session on YouTube before your first attempt. Hearing the rhythm and pacing demonstrated makes the first practice significantly more effective.

Do not use it as an emergency tool in the five seconds before you are called to speak. It requires time and stillness to work properly. Plan for it. Build it into your preparation the way you build in practice and structure — because regulation is not separate from preparation. It *is* preparation.

What Regulation Is Not

The goal is not to eliminate nervousness entirely.

A moderate level of activation is not your enemy. It sharpens focus. It adds energy and presence to your delivery. The greatest speakers in the world still feel it — the elevated heartbeat before they walk out, the heightened awareness in the first thirty seconds. What separates them from an untrained speaker is not the absence of that feeling.

It is what they do with it.

They regulate before they speak. They have trained their nervous system to discharge excess activation and arrive at the threshold ready — not flat, not panicked, but *poised.*

Understanding that nervousness is biological removes something that holds most people back more than the nervousness itself: self-blame. You are not weak for feeling it. You are not broken. You are not less capable than the person beside you who appears calm.

You are simply human. And now you have the tools to work with your biology instead of against it.

The next chapter takes this further — into what happens during speech itself. Because once you begin speaking, one tool above all others determines whether your voice remains steady or collapses under pressure. That tool has been with you since the moment you were born. You have simply never been taught to use it deliberately.

It is your breath

Chapter 6

Breath Is Power

In 2009, a 23-year-old named James entered the final round of a national debate competition. He had made it further than anyone from his university in years. His research was thorough. His arguments were sharp. His structure was clean. Everyone who had watched him in earlier rounds agreed: this was his competition to win.

He walked to the podium. The first minute was strong. Then, mid-argument, something shifted. His sentences began running into each other. His voice, which had been clear and steady, started thinning toward the ends of his words. He pushed harder, spoke faster, tried to compensate with energy. By the final thirty seconds, he was visibly straining. He finished. The room applauded politely.

The judges gave the win to his opponent. In their feedback, one line stood out above everything else. It did not mention his research or his logic or his vocabulary.

It said: he lost control of his delivery in the second half.

James spent weeks trying to understand what had gone wrong. He reviewed the recording dozens of times. And eventually, he noticed something he had never paid attention to before. Halfway through his argument, he had stopped breathing properly. Not dramatically. Not obviously. Just quietly, gradually, his breath had become shallow. His sentences had grown longer than his air supply could support. And his voice, starved of the one thing it runs on, had simply begun to collapse.

He had not lost the debate because of what he said. He had lost it because of how he breathed.

What Actually Produces Your Voice

Most people think the voice lives in the throat. It does not. The throat is simply the exit. The voice is powered from much further down.

Below your lungs sits the diaphragm, a wide dome-shaped muscle that most people have never consciously used in their lives. When you inhale deeply, the diaphragm contracts and pulls downward, creating space for the lungs to fully expand. When you exhale, it releases slowly and steadily, pushing a controlled stream of air upward. Your vocal cords vibrate against that stream. Your voice rides on it.

This is the mechanism. Speech is airflow made audible.

When breathing is shallow and chest-based, the airflow becomes thin and inconsistent. Thin airflow produces unstable vibration. Unstable vibration is what the listener hears as a shaky voice, fading volume, or a strained, pressured quality that signals anxiety even when the words themselves are confident.

Strong breath support does not mean speaking loudly. It means speaking on a steady, controlled stream of air. Steady airflow creates steady vibration. Steady vibration creates vocal authority. And vocal authority is what makes a listener lean in rather than check out.

The Two Mistakes Almost Everyone Makes

The first mistake is speaking on an empty tank. A shallow inhale, then speaking until the air runs out, then rushing the final words of the sentence to finish before oxygen does. The listener hears it as hurried and unstable, even if they cannot name why.

The second mistake is subtler. Some speakers take a deep breath and begin speaking immediately at the peak of inhalation, while the chest is still expanded and tense. At that peak, the throat tightens. The body is rigid. The voice arrives strained rather than free.

The correct approach sits between these two extremes, and it is simpler than most people expect.

Inhale deeply. Let a small amount of air release first. Then begin speaking on the smooth, controlled flow of the exhale. Not at the top of the breath, not scraping the bottom of it, but riding the steady middle of it. That is where the voice is most stable. That is where authority lives.

Sentence Length and Breath Capacity

There is a relationship between nervousness and sentence length that most speakers never notice until someone points it out.

When anxious, people instinctively make their sentences longer. It feels like they need to keep talking to maintain control. But longer sentences require more air. More air means deeper breathing. And when anxiety has already shortened the breath, long sentences become a problem the voice cannot solve.

If you regularly run out of air before a sentence ends, the sentence is too long for your current breath capacity. This is not a permanent limitation. It is a signal. Shorten the sentence. Pause. Breathe. Continue.

Short, controlled sentences do not sound simple. They sound authoritative. The pause between them is not emptiness. It is punctuation that the voice delivers. It tells the listener: that point is complete. A new one is coming. Stay with me.

So I was sitting in a speech competition once — not as a judge, not as a spectator, but as a participant waiting for my turn — and I had the kind of front row seat to human communication that you cannot manufacture in a classroom.

There were many participants that day. Different ages, different styles, different levels of preparation. Some had clearly rehearsed for days. Others were winging it with the quiet confidence of people who had done this before. What struck me — and I mean genuinely struck me, in a way that changed how I understood everything I had been reading about voice and delivery — was how consistently the same thing happened to speaker after speaker regardless of how prepared they appeared to be.

They would begin well. Strong opening. Clear first sentence. You could feel the room settle in. And then somewhere between the sixty and ninety second mark, something would quietly shift. The breath would shorten. The sentences would begin running longer than the air supply could support. The final words of each idea would arrive thin — not dramatically, not in a way most people in the audience could name, but in a way the room felt without knowing why. The energy would drop slightly. Attention would drift slightly. And the speaker, sensing the drift, would push harder and speak faster — which shortened the breath further and made everything worse.

I watched this pattern repeat across participant after participant. Not because they lacked intelligence or preparation or things worth saying. Because nobody had taught them that the voice is not a feature of the mouth. It is a product of the breath. And when the breath goes, everything built on top of it goes with it.

Then came the winner.

She was not the loudest speaker in the room. She was not the most dramatic or the most expressive. What she had was something I could see from where I was sitting — a steadiness in the way she managed her air that made every other speaker look like they were rationing a resource that was running out.

Every word of every sentence arrived with the same strength as the first. Not louder. Steadier. She did not rush the ends of her ideas. She did not strain toward her conclusion. The breath was the quiet infrastructure beneath everything she said — invisible to most people in the room, and absolutely responsible for every impression she created. The judges gave her the win and talked about clarity, composure, and authority. They never used the word breath. But watching her from five seats away, I knew exactly what they were actually responding to.

The runner-up was a genuinely gifted storyteller. Her language was vivid. Her structure was compelling. Her material was arguably more interesting than the winner's. But her breath was inconsistent. The peaks of her delivery were excellent. Between those peaks the air was thinning. And a voice that fades between its best moments cannot hold the impression those moments create. We will come back to her body language in the chapters ahead — because that was working against her too. But the breath was the primary gap between first and second place that day.

The difference was not intelligence. Not vocabulary. Not the quality of their ideas.

It was the ability to deliver the last word of a sentence with the same breath support as the first.

And then my name was called.

I had prepared for over twenty hours. Written the speech, refined it, timed it, rehearsed it until the words felt like they belonged to me rather than to a page. There was just one problem I had not noticed until the instructor stood up to brief the room right before the first participant was called.

Each speaker had three to five minutes.

I had prepared a ten-minute speech.

The instruction sheet had said the speech should be between three to five minutes. I had read it as at least three to five minutes — meaning I had spent twenty hours preparing twice times more content than the competition had space for. I was the fifth participant, which meant I sat through four complete speakers carrying that information in my chest before my name was called.

What followed was not my finest moment. I stood at that podium with a ten minute speech and approximately four minutes to deliver it, and the gap between those two numbers was not something I could bridge with skill or breath control or any other tool I had learned.

But I remember thinking — even in that moment — that the winner had still won. That her breath had still carried every word with the same strength from the first sentence to the last. That the lesson I had been watching from the fifth seat was real regardless of what was happening to me at the podium.

The competition taught me two things. One about breath. One about instructions.

Read every instruction twice. Slowly. Before you assume you have understood it.

Everything else in this chapter is about the first lesson — and that one, unlike misreading a sheet of paper, is a skill you can actually build before the next time your name is called.

The Micro-Reset

During any high-pressure speaking moment, breath will shorten. This is not failure. This is biology, and you already understand why it happens. Your job is not to prevent the shortening. Your job is to reset quickly when it occurs.

The technique is this: the moment you feel your breath becoming shallow mid-answer, pause. Inhale slowly and fully through the nose. Let a small amount be released. Then resume speaking.

Two seconds. That is all it takes.

The silence during that breath is not a weakness. Every person in the room reads it as the opposite. It reads as someone who is comfortable enough to pause. Someone who is in no rush. Someone who owns the space they are standing in.

Strong speakers pause to breathe. Speakers who are struggling rush to hide what they need to.

The audience always knows the difference. They may not know why one speaker feels more commanding than another. But they feel it. And breath is the invisible wire behind that feeling.

Training Breath Stability: Three Core Drills

Breath control is not a talent. It is a trainable physical skill, the same way a musician trains finger strength or a runner trains lung capacity. These three drills, practised consistently for five minutes a day, will build the breath foundation that every other communication skill in this book depends on.

The Equal Counting Drill trains consistency. Take one full deep breath. Exhale slowly while counting aloud, one number per beat: 1, 2, 3, 4, 5, and so on. Continue until the air runs out naturally. The goal is that every number receives the same vocal strength as the first. Most people begin strongly and fade noticeably by the fourth or fifth count. That fade is the problem this drill corrects. Repeat five times each session. Within two weeks, the difference will be audible.

The Extended Sentence Drill trains endurance and pacing. Take a full breath. Speak one complete, medium-length sentence on a single controlled exhale. Pause. Reset your breath fully. Speak the next sentence. The pause between sentences is part of the drill, not a break from it. You are training the habit of breathing between ideas rather than pushing through without air.

The Controlled Pause Drill trains coordination between ideas and breath. Take any paragraph from any book. Read it aloud. After every full stop, insert a deliberate breath pause before continuing. This feels slow at first. It will not sound slow to anyone listening. What it sounds like is someone who thinks in complete, finished thoughts. Which is exactly the impression you want to create.

One Rule From Here Forward

Before every important answer, inhale properly. Before introducing a key idea, reset your breath. Before your conclusion, check that your airflow is stable enough to carry you through the final sentence with the same strength as the first.

Breath is invisible. Your audience will never see it, comment on it, or consciously notice it.

But they will feel everything it does to your voice. Every word you speak rides on it. Every impression you create is shaped by it.

James went back to competition the following year. Same preparation, same research, same arguments. One thing changed. He trained his breath for eight weeks before the event. He won.

Not because he had better ideas. Because his voice finally had the power to carry them.

Part IV: Voice and Presence

Most communication training stops at what you say.

This section is about something deeper — how it arrives.

Two people can speak the same sentence, with the same structure, using the same vocabulary, and create completely different impressions in the room. One sounds uncertain and hurried. The other sounds composed and intentional. The content is identical. The perception is not.

That gap is not created by language. It is created by control. Control over pace, pause, tone, and presence. You are no longer correcting mistakes from this point forward. You are learning to shape how you are perceived before your content is even fully processed.

That is what this section is about.

HOW POWERFUL
IS YOUR VOICE?

Chapter 7

Pause as Authority

On the 8th of November, 1960, John F. Kennedy won the United States presidential election by one of the narrowest margins in American history. Political analysts spent years studying what separated him from his opponent Richard Nixon in the television debates that preceded it. They compared policies, appearance, vocabulary, and preparation.

But one pattern kept emerging in the research.

Kennedy paused. Nixon rushed.

PERSONALITY PROFILE

John F. Kennedy

1917 – 1963 • United States

35th President of the United States and one of the most studied communicators in political history. Kennedy's 1960 televised debate against Richard Nixon changed the course of an election and permanently altered how the world understood the relationship between presence, appearance, and spoken words.

COMMUNICATION LESSON

Kennedy used the pause as a tool of authority. He never rushed to fill silence. Each pause before a key phrase told the audience — what comes next matters. Slow down and listen.

Watch the footage today and it is immediately visible. When a difficult question landed, Kennedy would stop. Sometimes for a full two seconds. He would hold the silence with complete composure, as though the question had not rattled him at all. Then he would speak, measured and deliberate, each sentence arriving with the weight of someone who had chosen his words rather than scrambled for them.

Nixon, by contrast, filled every gap. The moment a question ended, the answer began. There was no space, no stillness, no moment where the listener could feel that something important was being considered. His words were not weak. His knowledge was not inferior. But the absence of pause made him appear reactive, unsettled, and somehow less certain even when he was certain.

Kennedy did not win the debate with better arguments.

He won it with better silence.

PERSONALITY PROFILE

Richard Nixon

1913 - 1994 • United States

37th President of the United States and one of the most consequential cautionary tales in the history of political communication. Nixon lost the 1960 presidential election to John F Kennedy – not on policy, not on argument, but on presence. Those who heard the debate on radio thought Nixon won. Those who watched it on television thought Kennedy won.

COMMUNICATION LESSON

Nixon arrived at the debate pale, sweating, and visibly uncomfortable under studio lights. His body communicated defeat before he spoke a word. What the audience sees always overrides what the speaker says.

What Rushing Actually Signals

There is an illusion that speed creates, and most speakers fall for it completely.

Rushing feels productive. It feels like fluency. It feels like you are covering ground, demonstrating knowledge, filling the space with capability. From the inside, it feels like confidence.

From the outside, it sounds like fear.

When a speaker rushes, the listener does not think: this person knows a great deal. The listener feels something more instinctive than that, something they may not even consciously articulate. They sense that the speaker is afraid of silence. Afraid that if they stop, someone will notice the gap. Afraid that stillness means emptiness.

And that fear, transmitted through pace, undermines every intelligent thing that follows.

Pause communicates the opposite. When you stop, deliberately and calmly, before answering a question or after delivering an important idea, you send a signal that no vocabulary can manufacture. You signal that you are not afraid of this moment. That you are not running from the silence. That you own the space you are standing in.

Control is not demonstrated by how much you say. It is demonstrated by how comfortable you are saying nothing.

The Three Things a Pause Does Simultaneously

When you pause intentionally, three things happen at once, and all three work in your favour.

Your breath stabilises. As we explored in the previous chapter, shallow breathing is the enemy of vocal authority. A deliberate pause gives the diaphragm time to reset. The next sentence arrives supported, steady, and clear.

Your thoughts realign. Mid-speech, the mind can drift ahead of the mouth or fall behind it. A pause closes that gap. It gives your thinking time to catch up with your delivery, so the next sentence begins from a place of clarity rather than recovery.

Your listener absorbs. Without pause, information stacks. Ideas arrive faster than the mind can file them, and the result is that nothing truly lands. With pause, each idea has a moment to settle before the next one arrives. The listener does not just hear more clearly. They remember more.

Pause is not empty space between words. It is the space where words become understood.

The Filler Word Problem

Most people believe filler words are a language problem. They are not. They are a silent problem.Um. Actually. Like. So. You know. Basically. These words do not appear because the speaker lacks vocabulary. They appear because the speaker is afraid of the gap that would exist without them. They are audible panic, a way of holding the floor while the brain searches for the next thought, a signal to the listener that says: I am still here, please do not look away, I have not finished yet.

But here is what those words actually communicate to the listener: I am not comfortable with silence. And a speaker who is not comfortable with silence is a speaker who does not fully trust themselves.

Replace the filler with nothing. Just stop. Let the silence sit for one second, two seconds if needed. The listener will not think you have forgotten. They will think you are thinking. And a speaker who thinks before speaking is infinitely more compelling than one who speaks to avoid thinking.

Silence sounds stronger than um. Every time.

I learned this lesson in a way I have never forgotten. During the first two weeks of college, our institution organised an induction programme for the new batch. Every day, teachers would come and talk about the journey ahead, the opportunities available, and what we could expect over the next four years. In the second half of the programme, senior students started joining the sessions and conducting activities designed to help us interact, participate, and step outside our comfort zones.

One of the activities was simple: stand up, introduce yourself, share a talent, tell a story, or say something to the group.

The first time they asked for volunteers, I stayed seated.

I watched other students participate while I remained silent. But when I returned to my room that evening, I made a decision. The next time an opportunity came, I would not let it pass. I did not want to leave college carrying the regret of all the moments I was too afraid to take.

So I prepared something.

I had written a shayari—my first original shayari. To make it meaningful, I planned to tell a short story before reciting it so that the audience would understand the context and feel the impact of the final lines.

The next day, when the seniors asked for volunteers again, I stood up.

My heart was racing, but I followed through with what I had planned. I told the story, recited the shayari, and sat down.

The response was better than I could have imagined.

The room applauded. Some students cheered. For a brief moment, I felt proud of myself—not because the performance was perfect, but because I had done something I would have avoided just twenty-four hours earlier.

Later that day, I asked a few friends what they remembered about my presentation.

I expected them to mention the story. Maybe the message. Maybe even the shayari itself. Instead, several of them said the same thing.

"What's it called...?"

I looked at them, confused.

"What do you mean?"

They laughed and repeated the phrase.

"What's it called... what's it called... what's it called..."

Only then did I realise what they were talking about.

Throughout the story, whenever I needed a moment to think, I had used the same filler phrase over and over again: *"What's it called..."*

The audience had enjoyed the presentation. They had appreciated the shayari. But one of the strongest memories they carried away was not my message. It was my filler word. That experience taught me something I have never forgotten.

Filler words do not merely fill silence. They compete with your message.

You may have a brilliant story, a powerful idea, or a creative piece of work. But if a filler word appears often enough, it starts drawing attention to itself. The listener stops focusing entirely on what you are saying and begins noticing how you are saying it.

My shayari deserved to be remembered.Instead, many people remembered the phrase I used while trying to avoid silence.

That is the true cost of filler words.

Three Pauses You Must Train

Not all pauses serve the same purpose. There are three types that every trained communicator uses deliberately.

The breath pause comes before an important sentence begins. It ensures that the diaphragm is loaded, that airflow is stable, and that the voice will carry the sentence from its first word to its last with equal strength. It also signals to the listener that something worth hearing is coming. Used before answering a significant question, it reads as composure. It reads as someone who is in no hurry because they do not need to be.

The idea pause comes after delivering a key point. It is perhaps the most powerful of the three. When you say something important and then immediately continue, you dilute it. The idea gets buried under what follows. When you say something important and then stop, the silence acts as a spotlight. It tells the listener: that was the point. Stay with it for a moment. The idea settles deeper because nothing came along to push it out.

The transition pause comes between one point and the next. Without it, sentences blur into each other and the structure you worked to build becomes invisible to the listener. With it, each section of your answer feels distinct and deliberate. The listener can feel the shape of what you are saying, not just the content.

Weak speakers pause by accident, when they run out of air or lose their thread.

Strong speakers pause on purpose, and the audience feels the difference without knowing why

The Surgeon and the Student

There is a story told in medical training circles about two surgeons performing the same procedure.

The first surgeon moves quickly and continuously throughout the operation. Every action follows the last with barely a breath between them. He finishes faster than anyone in his cohort. His colleagues admire his efficiency.

The second surgeon pauses at each critical juncture. Before making an incision, she stops. Looks. Check once more. Then act. Her procedures take slightly longer. But her outcomes are consistently better. Her error rate is significantly lower. And the nurses who work with her say the same thing: she makes the room feel calm.

Years later, a junior doctor asked her about it. She said something that had nothing to do with surgery but everything to do with the way she had trained herself to think.

She said: the pause is not where I lose time. The pause is where I make the decision.

Communication works on the same principle. The moment before you speak is not wasted time. It is decision time. It is where you choose what matters, how to begin, and how to land. Speakers who skip that moment do not save time. They simply make their decisions in public, under pressure, with the listener watching. And it shows.

Exercise : Training the Pause

Take any paragraph from any book, this one included. Read it aloud at your normal pace. Then read it again with these deliberate insertions: a one-second pause after every full stop, and a two-second pause after any sentence that contains a key idea.

Record both versions and listen back.

The second version will feel exaggerated to you. It will not sound exaggerated to anyone listening. What it will sound like is a person who is in complete control of what they are saying and in no rush to be anywhere else.

Do this for five minutes each day for two weeks. You are not practising reading. You are training a reflex. The reflex that reaches for stillness instead of filler. The reflex that trusts silence rather than fears it.

When that reflex becomes automatic, something changes in the room every time you speak. People lean in rather than drift. They wait for your next sentence rather than anticipating when you will finish. They do not know why. You will.

Because authority does not announce itself.

It simply pauses.

And let the room notice.

CHAPTER 8

Your Voice Is an Instrument

In 1963, a 34-year-old Baptist preacher stood on the steps of the Lincoln Memorial in Washington DC and delivered a speech to 250,000 people gathered below him and millions more watching on television screens across America.

He had prepared remarks. He had structure. He had an argument.

But somewhere in the middle of that speech, gospel singer Mahalia Jackson, standing just behind him, called out: "Tell them about the dream, Martin."

He paused. Pushed his notes aside. And then he spoke from something deeper than preparation.

PERSONALITY PROFILE

Martin Luther King Jr

1929 – 1968 • United States

Baptist minister, civil rights leader, and the most celebrated orator of the twentieth century. King's 1963 "I Have a Dream" speech delivered to 250,000 people at the Lincoln Memorial is a school of communication on inspiration, moral vision, and justice. He had the skill to lift hearts to see a world as it can be, the grace to be patient, and the structure to make every word carry the life of a vision.

> **COMMUNICATION LESSON**
>
> *King used rhythm and moral contrast like thread down a clear, common message when even ordinary speakers need to lead. The difference isn't in your role or audience — it's in the structure that reaches a better view.*

What followed was not just words. It was a voice that rose and fell like music, that slowed to a near-whisper at moments of gravity and swelled at moments of vision, that carried grief and hope in the same sentence through nothing more than the way the air moved through one man's body.

Martin Luther King Jr. did not have a perfect voice in the technical sense. What he had was complete mastery of it. Pitch, pace, resonance, rhythm, energy — every element working together with such precision that fifty years later, people who were not alive when he spoke can still feel something when they hear the recording.

That is what a trained voice does. It does not just carry words. It carries meaning.

Voice Is Not Personality. It Is Physiology.

The first thing to understand about the voice is that it is not a fixed feature of who you are. Most people believe their voice is simply the voice they were born with, the natural expression of their personality, unchangeable and unchosen.

This is incorrect.

Voice is physiology shaped by habit. It is the product of airflow, muscle coordination, resonance space, and articulation — all of which are trainable. Just as a musician does not simply play the instrument, they were born holding, a speaker does not have to keep the voice they have been unconsciously using for years.

Two speakers can say the exact same sentence with identical structure and vocabulary. One sounds flat, forgettable, slightly strained. The other sounds grounded, clear, and compelling. The words are the same. The voice is not. And the listener will trust the second speaker more before the content has even been fully processed.That is how much voice shapes perception.

The Physics Behind the Sound

Your voice begins with breath. Air rises from the lungs, passes through the vocal cords, and causes them to vibrate. That vibration produces sound. The sound then travels through resonance cavities in the throat, mouth, and nasal passages, where it gains depth, richness, and character before leaving the body.

Every stage of this journey matters.

If airflow is unstable, vibration becomes unstable. If muscles are tight, resonance becomes restricted. If articulation is lazy, clarity disappears at the final stage. Voice is not simply sound. It is coordinated airflow, vibration, resonance, and articulation working together. When one element weakens, the listener feels it, even if they cannot name it.

This is why vocal training is not about trying to sound different. It is about removing the obstacles that prevent your voice from carrying its full natural authority.

Monotone: The Hidden Authority Killer

There is a particular kind of speaker that audiences find almost impossible to stay with. Their content may be strong. Their structure may be clear. Their knowledge may be genuine. But within three minutes, the room has quietly drifted.

The cause, almost always, is monotone delivery.

Monotone speech is not caused by a lack of emotion or personality. It is caused by muscular rigidity — vocal cords operating in a narrow, restricted pitch range because they have never been trained to do otherwise. When pitch does not vary, the brain receives no signals about what matters more than something else. Everything sounds equally important, which means nothing sounds important at all. Listener engagement drops. Attention drifts.

Under stress, the problem compounds. A pitch range that is already narrow narrows further under pressure, which is precisely when you need it most.

Pitch flexibility must be trained. And the most effective tool for training it is something that has been used by professional singers and broadcasters for

decades.
I learned the impact of monotone delivery through one of my podcast episodes.

Before the recording, I was genuinely excited. The guest was a highly accomplished professional and the episode was the first of its kind on my channel. I expected it to be one of the most engaging conversations I had published.

But a few minutes into the recording, I noticed something unusual.

The answers were intelligent. The information was valuable. The experience behind the words was undeniable. Yet something was not landing the way I expected.

The delivery remained almost unchanged from beginning to end. The pitch rarely varied. Important ideas sounded similar to ordinary details. Stories, insights, and explanations were all delivered in nearly the same vocal range.

At the time, I could sense the issue, but I could not stop the conversation and ask the guest to change the way he spoke. Out of respect, I completed the recording, edited the episode, and published it as planned.

Then the audience responded.

The feedback was fascinating. People were not criticising the guest's knowledge. In fact, many acknowledged that the information was valuable. Yet a common theme appeared repeatedly. Viewers said the episode felt difficult to stay engaged with. Some could not explain why. Others simply said that something felt flat compared to other conversations on the channel.

What they were noticing was monotone delivery.

Most listeners do not know the technical term for it. They simply feel its effects. Their attention drifts. Their mind begins to wander. Information that should feel important arrives with the same weight as everything else.

That experience taught me an important lesson. Expertise does not automatically create engagement.

A person may spend years mastering medicine, engineering, law, business, or any other demanding profession. Yet the moment they begin speaking, people form impressions long before they evaluate the quality of the ideas being presented.

Fair or unfair, listeners judge the message through the voice delivering it.

Monotone speech does not reduce intelligence. It reduces the audience's ability to feel the intelligence behind the words.

And that is why vocal variety is not a performance skill. It is a communication skill.

The Siren Technique

Find a quiet space. Take a steady breath. Then glide your voice smoothly from a low comfortable hum up to a higher tone, and then back down, like the sound of a distant siren. Keep the airflow steady throughout. Do not force the sound. Do not chase volume. The goal is a smooth, unbroken transition across as wide a range as feels natural.

What this does physiologically is stretch and contract the vocal cords across their full usable range, building muscular coordination and reducing the stiffness that creates monotone delivery. It is the vocal equivalent of stretching before physical exercise. Without it, the cords operate in whatever restricted range habit has assigned them. With consistent practice, that range expands, and with it, the expressive capacity of everything you say.

Practice for two minutes each morning. Professional broadcasters do this before every live recording. The discipline is not complicated. The results are not subtle.

Lip Trills

This exercise looks undignified. It is extraordinarily effective.

Blow a steady stream of air through relaxed, loosely closed lips until they vibrate with a motorboat sound. Keep the airflow consistent. Add gentle pitch variation as you grow comfortable. Do this for one minute before any speaking practice.

What lip trills do is force sound production without throat tension. Many speakers, particularly under pressure, unconsciously tighten the throat in an attempt to control the voice. The result is the opposite of control. Tightness constricts resonance, strains the cords, and produces exactly the thin, pressured quality that signals nervousness to the listener.

Lip trills make throat tension physically impossible. The vibration can only be sustained through relaxed, breath-supported airflow. Every time you practise them, you are training the body to produce voice the right way and building a muscle memory that carries into actual speech.

Soft Palate Activation

Begin a gentle yawn, but stop halfway through. Notice what happens in the back of your mouth. There is a lifting sensation, a spaciousness that opens up behind your tongue. That is your soft palate rising.

When the soft palate lifts, the resonance chamber of the mouth expands. Sound has more space to develop before it leaves the body. The result is a fuller, richer, more authoritative tone without any increase in volume or effort.

When the soft palate remains low, which is its default position for most people in most conversations, sound becomes nasal, thin, or flat. The voice that arrives at the listener's ear carries less weight than the thought that produced it.

Practise this awareness daily. Begin a gentle yawn to feel the lift, then without completing the yawn, speak a short sentence in that open position. Notice the difference in quality. Over time, with consistent practice, the soft palate begins to lift naturally during speech, and the voice gains a depth that no amount of vocabulary or structure can substitute.

Over-Articulation: Building Muscle Memory

Most unclear speech is not a thinking problem or a language problem.

It is a muscular problem.

Under pressure, the jaw tightens. The lips move minimally. Consonants blur into each other. Words that were clear in the mind arrive at the listener's ear as something slightly less than intended.

The solution is deliberate exaggeration during practice. Open the mouth wider than feels comfortable. Strike each consonant with intention. Stretch the vowels beyond what seems necessary. Train at a level of precision that feels theatrical in private so that controlled, natural clarity becomes automatic in public.

Tongue twisters serve this purpose precisely because they demand muscular precision at a level that ordinary speech does not. Practise these slowly, with complete attention to each sound:

Red leather, yellow leather. Unique New York. She sells seashells by the seashore.

Speed is irrelevant. Precision is everything. Move the lips fully. Keep the breath steady. Let each sound be deliberate.

The muscle memory built in these slow, exaggerated sessions is what produces natural clarity under pressure. You are not practising tongue twisters. You are conditioning the articulatory muscles that carry your message from thought to sound.

Energy Generosity

There is a mistake that many intelligent, self-aware speakers make, particularly those who are afraid of appearing dramatic or over-confident.

They under-speak.

They suppress vocal energy in the belief that restraint reads as sophistication. What it actually reads as is hesitation. Low energy speech feels uncertain to the listener, regardless of how strong the content is. The voice signals commitment before the words are processed. A voice without energy suggests a speaker without conviction.

Energy in voice is not volume. It is not performance. It is the combination of consistent breath pressure, active facial muscles, dynamic pitch variation, and genuine emotional engagement with what you are saying. It is the difference between speaking at your material and speaking through it.

Train at a hundred and twenty percent intensity in private. Speak louder than necessary. Vary pitch more than feels natural. Commit to every sentence as though it matters. Then deliver at eighty percent in public settings. What feels like eighty percent to you will feel like a hundred percent to your listener, because most people are operating at fifty.

The Daily Vocal Conditioning Protocol

This ten-minute routine, practised consistently, builds the vocal foundation that every other communication skill in this book depends on.

One minute of humming with lips closed, feeling the vibration in the chest and face. This builds resonance awareness.

Two minutes of lip trills, with steady airflow and gentle pitch variation. This releases throat tension and trains breath support.

Two minutes of siren slides, moving smoothly from low to high and back. This builds pitch flexibility and reduces monotone tendencies.

Two minutes of slow, deliberate tongue twisters with exaggerated articulation. This conditions the muscles that produce clarity.

Three minutes of structured speaking at full energy, using frameworks from earlier chapters. This integrates everything into real delivery.

Do not train only before presentations. Train daily. Consistency is what moves a skill from conscious effort to automatic expression. The voice you use five years from now is being shaped by what you practise today.

The Final Principle

Content creates knowledge.

Voice creates perception.

Perception determines influence.

But even a perfectly trained voice does not operate alone. Your body is speaking before your mouth opens. Your posture, your facial expression, the way you hold yourself in space — these either reinforce your message or quietly contradict it. A voice built on everything in this chapter can still lose impact if the body signals hesitation, withdrawal, or disconnection.

In the next section, we move from what the ear receives to what the eye sees. Because communication is not only heard.

It is seen. It is felt. And it is believed or doubted before a single word lands.

PART V

BODY & EMOTIONAL TRANSMISSION

Before you speak, your body already has.

An audience reads your posture before your first word. They notice the tension in your face before your logic. They watch your hands before they hear your message. All of this happens in the first few seconds, often below conscious awareness.

Humans evolved to read physical signals long before language existed. Confidence, fear, openness, hesitation — these were survival cues interpreted instantly through the body. That instinct still operates in every classroom, boardroom, and conversation today.

Because of this, communication cannot be separated from the body delivering it.Your structure may be clear and your preparation strong, but if your posture collapses, your gestures scatter, or your expressions contradict your words, the message loses something vocabulary cannot repair.

That missing element is believability. This section is not about acting confident. It is about alignment. When your body, voice, and thought move in the same direction, credibility does not need to be declared — it is simply felt. When they conflict, no amount of eloquence can restore it.

WHAT IS YOUR BODY SAYING?

CHAPTER 9

Posture & Alignment

In 2012, a Harvard psychologist named Amy Cuddy walked onto a TED stage and told the audience something that seemed almost too simple to be true.

She and her colleagues had run a study in which participants were divided into two groups. One group held expansive, open postures — standing with feet wide apart, hands-on hips, chest lifted, chin level — for two minutes before a high-stakes mock job interview. The other group held contracted, closed postures — shoulders rounded, arms crossed, body folded inward — for the same two minutes. Neither group was told anything about confidence or performance. They were simply asked to hold a position and then walk into an interview room.

The evaluators who assessed those interviews — trained professionals who had no knowledge of the study's hypothesis and had not seen any of the posing — gave consistently higher marks to the participants who had held the expansive postures. Not because of what they said. Not because of their qualifications. Because of something in the way they carried themselves into the room.

Cuddy's TED talk went on to become one of the most watched in history — over forty million views. Her central argument was direct: your body language shapes not just how others see you, but how you experience yourself. The way you stand changes the way you think. The way you occupy space changes what you believe you are capable of.

Now here is what you deserve to know honestly. The hormonal claims in the original study — that power posing raises testosterone and lowers cortisol — have been disputed. Several attempts to replicate those specific findings produced inconsistent results. The biology is not settled.

But the behavioural finding has held. The interview evaluators still gave higher marks to the expansive posture group. The subjective experience of feeling more grounded, more present, and more capable after two minutes of open, aligned posture has been reported consistently — not just in research settings but by hundreds of thousands of people who have applied the principle in real situations.

Which means the practical lesson stands even where the precise mechanism is debated.

How you hold your body before and during a speaking situation changes how you are perceived. It also changes how you feel from the inside. And both of those things — perception and internal state — directly determine the quality of communication that follows.

This chapter is about understanding that mechanism and using it deliberately. Not performing confidence, you do not feel. Not adopting a pose and hoping for a hormone shift. But understanding the real, observable relationship between physical alignment and communicative authority — and building it into the way you prepare every time something important needs to be said.

PERSONALITY PROFILE

Amy Cuddy

Born 1967 • United States

Social psychologist and Harvard lecturer whose research on body language and power posing transformed how we understand confidence, presence, and performance.

COMMUNICATION LESSON

Your body prepares your mind before your words.
How you stand shapes how you think,
and how you think shapes how you communicate.

The Body Speaks First

Long before structured language evolved, human beings survived by reading physical signals. Expansion indicated strength. Contraction indicated vulnerability. Stillness suggested control. Erratic movement suggested instability. These instincts are ancient, and they have not left us simply because we now sit in offices and classrooms instead of open plains.

The audience in any room is reading your body before your first word leaves your mouth. They are not doing this consciously. Their nervous system is doing it automatically; the same way it has been doing it for thousands of years. Confidence, fear, openness, hesitation — all of these are registered physically within seconds of seeing a person stand up to speak.

This means that posture is not cosmetic. It is not something you attend to after sorting out your content, structure, and delivery. It is the first message your audience receives. And first messages shape everything that follows.

What Alignment Actually Is

Perfect posture is not stiff. It is not the rigid, military-straight spine that most people imagine when they hear the word. It is alignment — the natural stacking of the body's structure in a way that creates physiological advantage without tension.

When alignment collapses, breath collapses. When breath collapses, voice weakens. When the voice weakens, authority drops. The chain is direct and consistent. Posture is not separate from vocal power. It is the physical foundation on which vocal power stands. Alignment begins from the ground upward. Feet placed approximately shoulder-width apart — not so narrow that the body appears unstable, not so wide that it reads as aggression. Knees relaxed, never locked. The spine lengthened upward naturally, without forcing. The chest opening without being artificially pushed forward. The neck sitting above the shoulders rather than leaning forward toward the listener.

This structural neutrality does something beyond appearance. When the chest expands properly, lung capacity increases. Increased lung capacity supports steady breath. Steady breath supports a stable voice. And a stable voice, as we have already established, is where authority lives.

Research in embodied cognition adds another layer to this. When the body expands slightly, the brain receives feedback that the environment is safe. Internal threat signals reduce. The speaker feels less defensive, less anxious, more grounded. Alignment therefore does not only change how others see you. It changes how you experience yourself while speaking. The body and the mind are in continuous conversation, and posture is one of the clearest messages the body sends inward.

Finding Your Alignment

Before any important speaking situation, use this reset. Stand with feet shoulder-width apart. Look briefly upward toward the ceiling. Raise both arms overhead and stretch gently. Then release, allowing the arms to fall naturally while maintaining the length in the spine. Let the shoulders settle without collapsing. Bring the gaze forward to eye level.

Notice what changed. The chest opened. The spine lengthened. The head found its position above the shoulders rather than ahead of them. This is structural neutrality. It takes four seconds. It changes the entire physical message you are sending.

A second practice is video observation. Record yourself speaking for one minute. Then watch the recording with the sound off. Without the distraction of words, the body becomes impossible to ignore. Watch whether the shoulders collapse mid-sentence. Watch whether the weight shifts repeatedly from foot to foot. Watch whether the head drifts forward as the effort of speaking increases. Removing audio forces an honest confrontation with physical coherence.

The Power Sphere

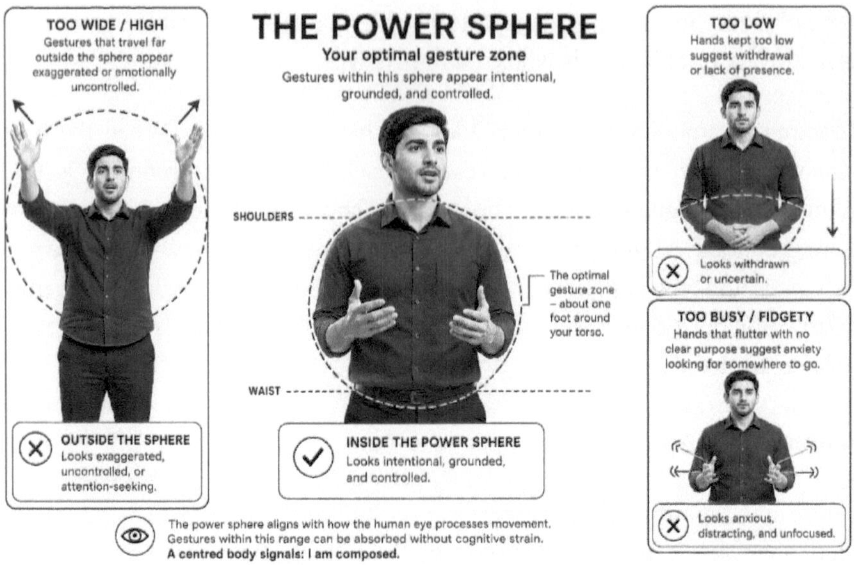

Within aligned posture operates a zone that experienced communicators instinctively understand and untrained speakers consistently violate.

Imagine an invisible sphere extending roughly one foot around your torso, bounded between the waist and the shoulders. This is the optimal gesture zone. Gestures that live within this sphere appear intentional, grounded, and controlled. Gestures that travel far outside it — hands flung upward or outward beyond comfortable range — appear emotionally uncontrolled or exaggerated. Hands kept too low suggest withdrawal. Hands that flutter with no clear purpose suggest anxiety looking for somewhere to go.

The power sphere works because it aligns with how the human eye processes movement. Gestures within this range can be absorbed without cognitive strain. The speaker appears centered. And a centered body signals to the audience, beneath conscious thought, that the person standing before them is composed.

The Language of Hands

Hands are psychological instruments. Their orientation, position, and movement change meaning before a single word is spoken. Most speakers never consciously think about their hands. And that is precisely why the hands so often betray what the mouth is trying to say.

Palm-up gestures communicate openness and invitation. They signal that the speaker is offering an idea rather than imposing one. This orientation lowers perceived threat in the listener and increases receptivity. Use it when explaining, when sharing perspective, when drawing the audience toward an idea rather than pushing it at them. The palm-up position is one of the oldest gestures of non-aggression in human history. It says: I am holding nothing. I am offering something.

Palm-down gestures communicate authority and finality. They work effectively when reinforcing a decisive point or signaling that a conclusion has been reached. A controlled downward press of the hands while delivering a final statement adds visible weight to the words. Used excessively however, they shift from authority into dominance, and dominance creates resistance rather than connection.

Placaters and Levelers

Two gesture patterns reveal more about a speaker's internal state than almost anything else.

Placater gestures are submissive, appeasing movements — palms raised excessively, hands held close to the chest, repeated upward motions that unconsciously communicate: I hope you agree with me. I am not looking for conflict. Please approve of what I am saying. These gestures appear most frequently when a speaker is afraid of disagreement or uncertain of their own position. The body attempts to reduce threat by signalling submission. In interviews, presentations, and negotiations, excessive placating quietly shifts power toward the audience and away from the speaker.

Leveler gestures are the opposite. Horizontal, steady movements with the palm facing downward or sideways, used to create balance and visual calm. They communicate: this is measured, this is stable, this is under control. Levelers are particularly effective during explanations and comparisons because they reduce emotional volatility in the visual field. The audience feels the steadiness of the gesture before processing the content of the words.

The most effective communicators move between these consciously. Openness when inviting. Authority when concluding. Balance when explaining. The hands become a second language that either reinforces the spoken message or quietly contradicts it.

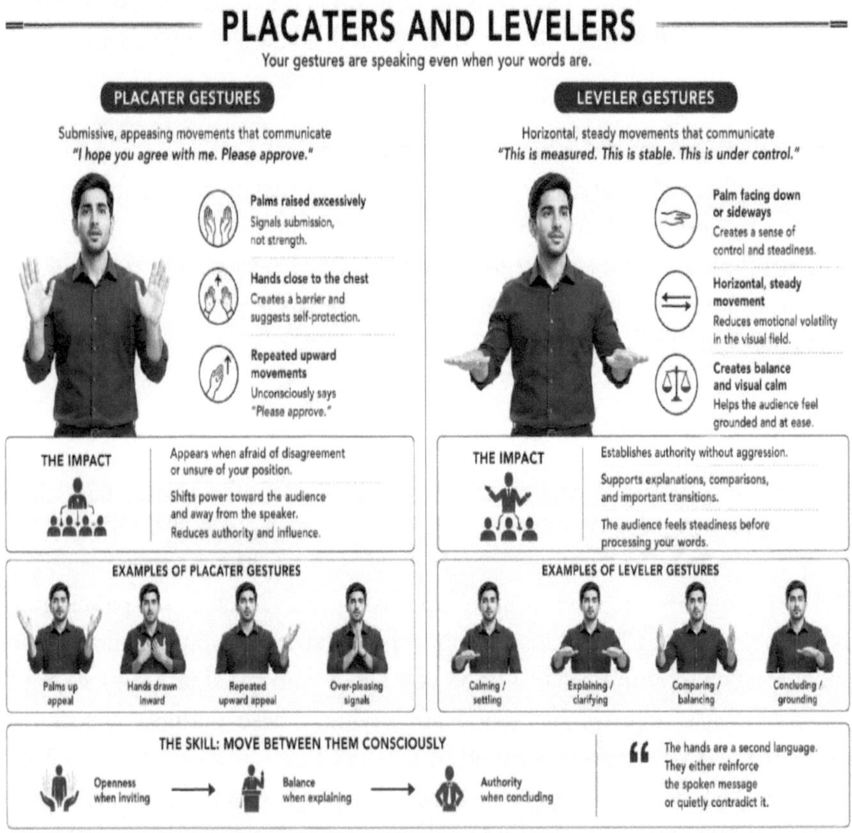

The Pointing Finger

Of all hand gestures, the pointing finger carries the sharpest psychological charge.

A direct finger-point, even when completely unintentional in its meaning, activates a defensive response in the listener. The instinct behind this reaction is ancient. Being pointed at historically preceded being singled out, accused, or targeted. The nervous system has not forgotten this, even in a classroom or a boardroom. Even when the speaker means nothing hostile by it, the pointed finger creates a subtle but measurable closing in the listener. They become less receptive. Slightly more defended.

Skilled communicators replace pointing with open-hand directional gestures. Rather than extending a single finger toward a person or an idea, the entire open hand guides the audience's attention in the intended direction. It achieves the same communicative purpose without triggering the defensive reflex. The message lands. The listener stays open.

The Thinking Gestures: Steeple and Cheek Rest

Not all-important gestures belong to the speaker. Some of the most valuable signals in any conversation come from the listener, and learning to read them changes how you communicate in real time.

The **steeple gesture** is formed when a person brings their fingertips together while keeping the palms apart. It is one of the most consistently recognised gestures in body language research. It signals confident, evaluative thinking. A listener who moves into a steeple position is processing what you said with genuine consideration. They are engaged. They are weighing your words. This is a positive signal. Continue with clarity and let the thought land.

The **cheek rest** is equally common but far more nuanced. The elbow rests on a table or armrest, the hand rises, and the cheek or jaw settles into the palm.

This gesture has two very different meanings depending on one detail.

When the index finger points upward along the cheek and the thumb supports the chin, it signals **critical evaluation**. The listener is actively judging your ideas and forming an opinion, possibly a sceptical one. This is not a signal to panic. It is a signal to strengthen your reasoning and provide clearer evidence.

When the full hand supports the head and the body leans heavily into the palm, the meaning changes entirely. It now signals **disengagement**. The listener is no longer actively evaluating. They have mentally stepped back from the conversation.

When you notice this as a speaker, resist the urge to speak louder or faster. Instead, pause. Ask a direct question. Change the pace. Create a moment that requires the listener to re-engage rather than simply receive.

Self-Touch Gestures

There is one final category of gesture that deserves attention because it appears so frequently under pressure.

Self-touch gestures are movements directed toward your own body rather than the audience: touching the face, adjusting clothing, running a hand through the hair, rubbing the neck, or pressing fingers to the lips. These gestures are not random. They are self-soothing behaviours. Under stress, the nervous system instinctively seeks physical comfort, and the body becomes the easiest source of that comfort. The challenge is that these gestures are visible to the audience, and they often communicate the same message: this person is managing discomfort right now. The goal is not to suppress every movement. Forced stillness creates its own tension. The goal is to return to neutral. When a gesture is complete, let the hands rest comfortably at your sides or in front of your body. They do not search for something to do. And rest, in a speaker's body, reads as one of the strongest signals of confidence. It reads as someone who does not need comfort because they are already comfortable.

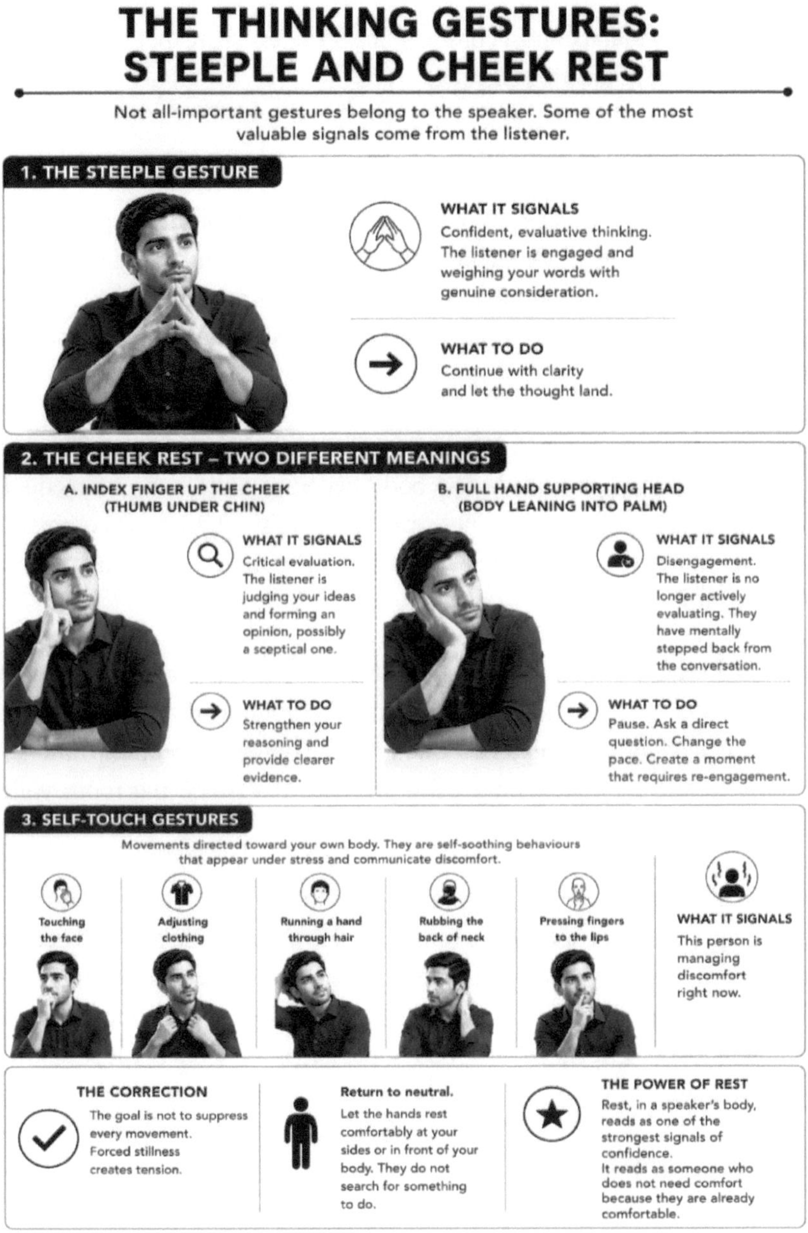

Stillness as Command

There is a quality that the most commanding speakers share that is almost never discussed in communication training.

They know when to stop moving.

Untrained speakers leak nervous energy continuously through repetitive hand motion, face touching, clothing adjustments, weight shifting, and gestures that serve no communicative purpose. These movements are not stylistic. They are stress indicators. The body is trying to discharge anxiety, and the audience reads every signal.

Controlled speakers return to neutral position between gestures. The hands settle. The feet stay grounded. The body becomes still at the moments that matter most. That stillness does not read as passivity. It reads as command. It tells the room that this person is not managing their anxiety through movement. They are simply present.

Ratan Tata was known for this quality throughout his career. Unlike many business leaders who dominated rooms through volume, dramatic gestures, or forceful displays of authority, Tata often did the opposite. People who worked with him frequently described a calm presence that filled the room without demanding attention.

During board meetings and high-level negotiations, he was not known for interrupting, pacing, or speaking over others. He listened. He allowed people to finish. When others rushed to fill silence, he was comfortable letting a pause exist. Colleagues often noted that when he finally spoke, the room paid attention—not because he was the loudest person present, but because his words were deliberate.

His stillness created contrast.

While others spent energy trying to appear powerful, Tata appeared comfortable enough not to prove anything. His movements were economical. His gestures were purposeful. His posture remained composed. As a result, even simple statements carried weight.

This is one of the paradoxes of communication. The more unnecessary movement you remove, the more impact your necessary movements have. A single gesture becomes noticeable. A pause becomes meaningful. A sentence becomes memorable.

Stillness is not the absence of presence.

It is concentrated presence.

PERSONALITY PROFILE

Ratan Tata

1937 - 2024 • India

Chairman Emeritus of Tata Sons and one of India's most respected industrialists. Under his leadership the Tata Group expanded from a national conglomerate into a global enterprise spanning over 100 countries. Known as much for his humility and stillness as for his business acumen, Ratan Tata commanded rooms without ever needing to dominate them.

COMMUNICATION LESSON

Ratan Tata never gestured for effect. His hands were calm, his posture open, his eye contact warm and unhurried. He demonstrated that the most powerful presence in any room is often the quietest one — because stillness signals that a person has nothing to prove.

Exercise 9: The Body Audit

Record yourself answering a question for two minutes. Then watch it twice.

The first time with sound, observing how your body supports or contradicts your words.

The second time without sound, watching only the body as though meeting this person for the very first time.

Ask yourself these questions honestly. Does this person look certain? Does the body reinforce the message or create a second, quieter message of its own? Which gestures served the communication and which ones leaked anxiety? Did the hands return to neutral or did they search continuously for somewhere to go?

Note three specific physical habits you observe. Not to judge them. To see them clearly. Because the body cannot be corrected until it has been honestly seen.

Alignment is not performance.

It is the physical expression of a prepared and present mind.

CHAPTER 10

Face, Eye Contact and Emotional Transmission

In May 1998, India conducted a series of nuclear tests at Pokhran in the Rajasthan desert. The operation had been carried out under extraordinary secrecy. Even many senior officials were unaware of the full details until the tests were complete. Within hours, the news spread across the world.

The announcement triggered immediate international reaction. Several countries condemned the tests. Economic sanctions were discussed. Foreign governments demanded explanations. News channels across the globe began analysing what the decision meant for regional stability and India's future role on the world stage.

Amid that atmosphere, one of the most anticipated press conferences in modern Indian history was organised. Journalists packed the room. Cameras pointed toward the stage. Millions of people waited for answers. The questions hanging in the air were larger than science. What would happen next? Had India taken a dangerous risk? How would the world respond?

When Dr. A.P.J. Abdul Kalam stepped forward to speak, the moment carried enormous pressure. He was not only representing a scientific achievement. In the eyes of many people, he was representing the confidence and credibility of the entire mission.

And yet the face of the man speaking carried something that softened the tension before a single technical explanation was given.

It carried calm.

Not the performed calm of someone suppressing anxiety. Not the rigid blankness of someone trying to appear unaffected. But the genuine, settled composure of a person who had complete internal clarity about what he believed and why.

His eyes were steady. His expression was measured. His posture remained relaxed. There was no visible conflict between what he was saying and what he was feeling. His face and his words communicated the same message.

That alignment matters more than most people realise.

The audience did not simply listen to the announcement. They unconsciously evaluated the messenger. Before people judge the logic of a message, they judge the emotional credibility of the person delivering it. Kalam's facial expressions communicated certainty without arrogance, confidence without aggression, and seriousness without fear.

The audience did not just hear the announcement.

They felt it was safe to trust it. That is what the face does. Long before the mind has processed the logic of what is being said, the face has already answered the most important question the audience is silently asking:

Can I trust this person?

PERSONALITY PROFILE

APJ Abdul Kalam

1931 – 2015 • India

A scientist, aerospace engineer, and the 11th President of India, known as the 'Missile Man of India.' Kalam's journey from a small town to Rashtrapati Bhavan inspired millions across generations. He combined a deep technical mind with a human heart, believing in youth leadership, the power of dreams, and the importance of education as the defense that lasts a lifetime.

COMMUNICATION LESSON

Kalam communicated with simplicity — the uncommon kind. His voice was soft, and his words were powerful. He never tried to impress; he tried to inspire. He spoke to the young as equals, transformed complex ideas into hope, and believed that the best future is built when the best minds are free.

The Neuroscience Behind What You Feel in a Room

In the 1990s, neuroscientists studying primates made a discovery that quietly changed our understanding of human connection. They found specialized brain cells, later called mirror neurons, that activated not only when a subject performed an action, but also when they simply observed someone else performing it. The brain, it turned out, does not sharply distinguish between doing and witnessing. It simulates both.

Further research extended this understanding into emotional experience. When we observe someone expressing tension, our own neural circuits partially recreate that tension. When we observe someone expressing calm, our circuits simulate calm. When we observe someone expressing joy, something in us responds before we have consciously decided to.

This is why a yawn travels across a room. This is why one anxious person in a group can raise the collective stress of everyone around them without saying a word. This is why certain leaders walk into a crisis and the room steadies, while others walk in and the room tightens further.

Emotional contagion is not metaphor. It is neurology. And it means that every time you stand up to speak, you are not only delivering information. You are transmitting an internal state. The audience absorbs it whether they intend to or not.

If your face shows fear, the room feels unstable. If your face shows composure, the room feels safe. The content you deliver rides on top of that emotional transmission, and it will only be trusted to the degree that the transmission beneath it feels true.

One of the clearest demonstrations of emotional transmission I have ever witnessed happened inside my own classroom.

During one semester of my B.Tech program, we had a new faculty member assigned to teach Internet and Web Designing (IWD). It was his first interaction with our class, and from the moment he walked into the room, something felt different.

He was clearly knowledgeable. He had earned the position and understood the subject. The problem was not his technical competence.

The problem was that his face, posture, and overall presence seemed completely overwhelmed by stress.

As he introduced himself, his facial expressions revealed nervousness. His body language lacked stability. His eyes rarely settled. Every movement seemed to communicate pressure rather than confidence.

What fascinated me was what happened to the classroom.

Within minutes, that emotional state spread to the students. The room felt heavy. Attention dropped. People became distracted. Conversations started. Many students, including me, found ourselves disengaging from the lecture even though the content itself was not necessarily poor.

Months later, I experienced the opposite.

Another professor was assigned to teach us Digital Electronics (DE). Before he even entered the classroom, he already had a disadvantage. He had missed several weeks of classes at the beginning of the semester, and many students had formed a negative impression of him before meeting him.

But the moment he walked into the room, the atmosphere changed.

His posture was relaxed. His movements were controlled. His eye contact was natural. There was no visible effort to appear confident because confidence was already present. He spoke with calm authority and complete comfort in his own skin.

Something remarkable happened.

Students who had been complaining about the missed classes forgot about them. Attention returned. Participation increased. The class became engaged. People began admiring not only the way he taught but also the way he carried himself.

Even today, many students say they would happily choose another course taught by him if given the opportunity.

The difference between these two teachers was not intelligence. Both were qualified educators.

The difference was the emotional experience they created the moment they entered the room.

One transmitted tension.

The other transmitted confidence.

And that is the lesson most people miss. Communication is not only about what people hear. It is also about what they feel in your presence. You may achieve success, earn degrees, build expertise, and collect credentials. But the impression people carry away from an interaction is often shaped less by what you know and more by the emotional state you consistently project.

Whether you intend to or not, your face, posture, and presence are teaching people how to feel about you long before they evaluate your words.

The Face Confirms or Contradicts

There is a reason audiences remember how a speaker made them feel long after they have forgotten what the speaker actually said.

The face processes and transmits emotional information faster than language processes logic. By the time your carefully structured argument has reached its conclusion, the audience has already made an emotional judgement about whether they believe you. That judgement was formed in the first few seconds of watching your face.

Micro-expressions are the mechanism behind this. These are involuntary facial movements lasting a fraction of a second — a tightening around the eyes, a brief compression of the lips, a barely perceptible raise of the eyebrows. Most people cannot consciously identify them. But the nervous system reads them fluently. And they reveal what is actually happening internally, regardless of what the words are claiming.

Tightened lips signal suppressed doubt. Rapid blinking signals internal stress. A jaw held rigid signals the effort of controlling something that wants to surface. A forced smile, where the mouth moves but the eyes do not follow, signals that the warmth being performed is not the warmth being felt.

You cannot eliminate micro-expressions through willpower. Attempting to control them consciously tends to increase rigidity, which creates its own visible signal. The only reliable path to facial authenticity is the one this book has been building toward from the beginning: regulate the internal state first. When breath is stable, when the nervous system is not in threat response, when the mind has structure and the body has alignment, the face follows naturally. It does not need to be managed because there is nothing left to conceal.

Eye Contact: The Most Intimate Communication Tool

Of all the physical elements of communication, eye contact is the most psychologically powerful and the most consistently mishandled.

Too little eye contact signals avoidance. The listener interprets it as insecurity, evasiveness, or a lack of conviction in what is being said. They begin to wonder what the speaker is not willing to look at directly. Trust quietly erodes.

Too much unbroken eye contact creates a different problem. Sustained, unvarying eye contact crosses from engagement into intensity, and intensity without warmth reads as aggression or dominance. The listener becomes uncomfortable. They begin to feel evaluated rather than communicated with.

The balance point is controlled variation.

In one-on-one conversation, maintain eye contact for three to five seconds at a time before looking away naturally — not downward, which signals submission, but slightly to the side, which signals thought. Then return. This rhythm communicates engagement without pressure.

In group settings, distribute eye contact deliberately. Move from person to person with each complete idea, not mid-sentence. When you begin a new point, find a new pair of eyes. This creates the experience for every individual in the room that you are speaking to them specifically, even in a group of fifty.

When answering a question, establish eye contact before you begin speaking. That moment of connection before the first word signals readiness and composure. When delivering your most important point, sustain the eye contact slightly longer than usual. The audience registers this lengthening instinctively. It tells them: this is the part that matters most.

The Indian Classroom

There is a cultural pattern worth addressing directly, because it affects a significant number of readers of this book.

In many Indian households and educational environments, prolonged eye contact with authority figures — teachers, parents, elders — is traditionally considered disrespectful. The instinct to look downward when addressed by someone senior is deeply conditioned from childhood. It is a gesture of humility and deference that carries genuine cultural respect within its original context.

The problem arises when that same conditioned reflex appears in professional and academic communication settings where the cultural context has shifted. In a job interview, a presentation, or a professional meeting, the same downward gaze that once communicated respect now communicates uncertainty. The interviewer across the table does not share the cultural context. They read the avoidance at face value.

This is not a criticism of cultural value. It is an awareness that communication requires reading the context you are in and adjusting accordingly. The respect you carry can remain internal. The eye contact you offer can be deliberate and confident. Both can coexist. Developing that ability — to carry cultural humility while projecting professional confidence — is itself a sophisticated communication skill.

Facial Neutrality and Controlled Expression

There are two common mistakes speakers make with facial expression, and they sit at opposite ends of the same problem.

The first is suppression. Some speakers, in an attempt to appear serious and professional, flatten their expression entirely. The face becomes a mask. No warmth, no responsiveness, no visible engagement with what they are saying. This does not read as seriousness. It reads as either anxiety being contained or indifference. Either way, the audience disconnects because the face is giving them nothing to connect with.

The second mistake is overcompensation. Exaggerated expressions, performed enthusiasm, smiles held too long beyond their natural duration. These read as inauthentic within seconds. The audience cannot always articulate why, but they feel the gap between what the face is performing and what the eyes are actually communicating.

The ideal state is controlled responsiveness. When the content is serious, the face reflects seriousness naturally. When something genuinely positive is being shared, a real smile emerges — one that involves the eyes as much as the mouth. Expression follows content rather than preceding it or contradicting it.

This alignment between face and message is what creates the experience of watching someone who is completely present in what they are saying. It is rare enough to be immediately compelling when it appears.

The Calm Projection Drill

Set your phone to record and place it at eye level. Deliver a two-minute response to any question from the exercises in previous chapters. Watch it back twice.

The first time with sound, observing how your face supports or contradicts your words.

The second time without sound, watching only your face as though you are meeting this person for the first time. Ask yourself the question your audience is always silently asking: does this person look like they believe what they are saying?

Note where the face tightened unnecessarily. Note where the eyes shifted at moments of uncertainty. Note where expression and content aligned, because those moments matter too. You are training awareness before correction. You cannot adjust what you have not clearly seen. Then repeat the exercise with one deliberate change. Before pressing record, take two full breaths. Reset posture. Find alignment. Then speak. Compare the recordings. The difference that two breaths and aligned posture make to facial expression is consistently larger than people expect.

The Three-Level Eye Contact Exercise

Level one is one-on-one practice. Speak with a partner or family member and consciously maintain eye contact for five full seconds before shifting naturally. Notice the instinct to look away before five seconds arrives. Stay with the discomfort until it becomes comfortable.

Level two is small group simulation. Present a two-minute structured response to three people seated in different positions. Deliver each complete idea to a different person. Do not rush eye contact. Let each person feel that the idea was delivered specifically to them.

Level three is camera training. Record yourself speaking directly into the lens without looking away. The camera is an unforgiving mirror for nervous eye movement. It reveals every shift, every avoidance, every moment of doubt that the eyes betray before the voice does. Practice until the lens no longer feels like a test. Until it feels like a conversation.

Emotional Responsibility

When you stand before an audience, you carry a responsibility that goes beyond the accuracy of your content.

You are responsible for the emotional atmosphere of the room.

This is not an exaggeration. It is a practical consequence of mirror neuron function. The internal state you bring into the room travels. If you are calm, the room stabilises around that calm. If you are chaotic, the room absorbs that chaos. If you are genuinely engaged with what you are saying, the audience finds it easier to be engaged. If you are simply performing engagement while internally disconnected, the audience feels that gap without being able to name it.

Emotional transmission is not optional. It is not something that happens only when you intend it. It is constant and unavoidable. The only question is whether you are transmitting it consciously or accidentally.

Regulate internally. Align externally. Transmit intentionally.

The face that does this consistently — the face that has been prepared through breath, posture, structure, and honest practice — is not performing confidence.

It has simply become it.

PART VI

STORYTELLING & INFLUENCE

Facts inform. Stories transform.

The most influential communicators across history were rarely the ones with the most information. They were the ones who made information feel personal. Because the human brain is not wired for isolated data. It is wired for narrative.

You may forget a statistic within hours. You rarely forget a story that made you feel something. When Martin Luther King Jr. spoke about equality, he did not list injustices. He narrated a dream. When Zakir Khan steps onto a stage, he does not open with a punchline. He opens with a moment — a hostel room, a late-night call home, a father's silence that said everything. The audience laughs, but more than that, they recognise themselves. And the moment a listener sees themselves inside your story, influence has already begun.

That is not talent. That is architecture.

Storytelling is a learnable, repeatable, trainable structure. The next two chapters will show you exactly how it works — and how to use it in every communication situation that matters to you.

Because facts can be ignored. A story that feels true connects.

DO YOUR STORIES WIN MINDS?

CHAPTER 11

The Structure of Powerful Stories

There is a moment in every great story where the audience stops being an audience.

They stop watching. They stop listening. They enter. The boundary between the teller and the listener dissolves, and what was someone else's experience becomes, for a few seconds, their own. When that happens, something shifts in the relationship between speaker and listener that no argument, no statistic, and no perfectly structured framework can replicate.

That moment is not accidental. It is engineered.

And the engineering is learnable.

Why the Brain Responds to Story

When you hear a fact, the language-processing regions of the brain activate. The information is decoded, filed, and in most cases, forgotten within hours.

When you hear a story, something entirely different happens. Multiple regions activate simultaneously — the sensory cortex begins simulating the physical environment of the scene, the emotional centers respond to the feelings of the characters, the motor areas partially recreate the actions being described. The brain does not just receive a story. It inhabits it briefly. And what we inhabit, we remember. What we remember, we believe. What we believe, we act on.

This is why storytelling builds empathy. Empathy builds trust. Trust enables influence. The chain is direct, and it begins the moment a listener stops processing information and starts experiencing narrative.Stories generate feelings. Feeling strengthens memory. Memory shapes belief.

The Architecture of a Powerful Story

Every strong story follows a clear internal progression. Not because storytelling is formulaic, but because this progression mirrors the way the human mind naturally seeks to make sense of experience.

Context grounds the listener in a specific place and time. Not background information — a scene. Where are we? Who is present? What does it feel like to be there?

Conflict creates tension. Without conflict, there is no story. There is only a description. Conflict is the engine. It is the moment something becomes uncertain, difficult, or at stake. The audience leans in because they do not yet know how this resolves.

Struggle humanizes the experience. This is where most untrained storytellers rush past the most valuable part. The struggle — the internal doubt, the external obstacle, the moment when the outcome was genuinely unclear — is where the audience finds themselves. They are not watching a hero. They are watching a human being. And they recognise the feeling.

Shift introduces transformation. Something changes — a decision is made, a realisation arrives, an unexpected event alters the direction. The shift is the hinge of the story. Everything before it creates tension. Everything after it carries the meaning.

Resolution provides closure. The brain seeks resolution the way the eye seeks a horizon. Without it, the audience feels incomplete. Resolution does not have to be triumphant. It simply has to be honest.

The lesson connects the story to meaning. Stories without reflection are diaries. Stories with reflection become influenced. The lesson does not need to be stated loudly or repeatedly. But it must be present. It is why the story was told.

Without conflict, there is no engagement. Without resolution, there is no impact. Without lessons, there is no influence.

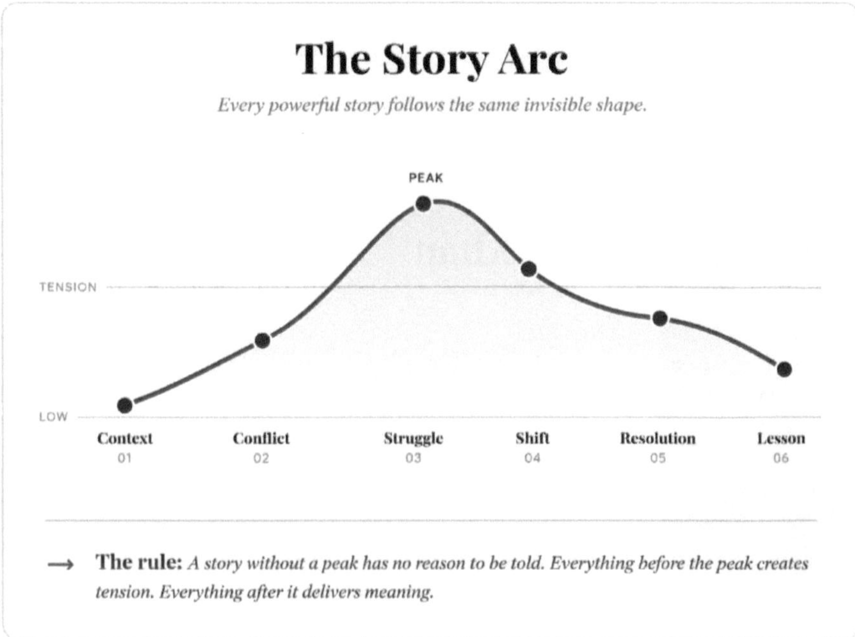

Zakir Khan: Structure Hidden in Laughter

Watch any long-form performance by Zakir Khan carefully and you will see this architecture operating beneath every laugh.

He begins with context — a specific, recognisable setting. Not "Indian families" in the abstract, but a particular evening, a particular room, a particular silence at the dinner table that every person in the audience has sat through. Then conflict arrives — parental expectations, academic pressure, the quiet weight of being compared to someone else's success. The struggle unfolds through vulnerability and self-awareness. He does not present himself as the winner of these moments. He presents himself as the person who felt exactly what the audience has felt.

Then the shift comes — an insight, a realisation, a moment where the absurdity of the situation reveals something true. The audience laughs because recognition strikes. And beneath the laughter, almost without noticing, a lesson has landed.

PERSONALITY PROFILE

Zakir Khan

Born 1987 • Indore, India

One of India's most beloved stand-up comedians, best known for his deeply personal storytelling style and the character of the Sakht Launda. Zakir does not tell jokes — he tells stories from his own life with such honest specificity that millions of people feel he is describing their own experience. His storytelling made him a cultural phenomenon across an entire generation.

COMMUNICATION LESSON

Zakir's power comes from specific personal detail, not general relatability. He does not say everyone feels lonely — he describes one exact evening, one exact feeling, one exact moment. Specificity is what makes a story universal.

What makes it powerful is not exaggeration. It is specificity. He does not say parents put pressure on us. He recreates the exact dialogue. He gives the father a particular tone of voice, the mother a specific expression, the moment a precise texture. The audience does not think about the story. They are inside it.

Specificity creates immersion. Immersion creates identification. Identification builds influence.

The Difference Between Information and Story

Information says: confidence is important for career success.

The story says: a student prepared for six months, answered every practice question perfectly, walked into the interview room, and froze completely when the first question was asked. He knew the answer. His body did not cooperate. He left without the job and spent three weeks wondering what had gone wrong.

Information informs. The story illustrates. Illustration persuades.

When Nelson Mandela spoke of reconciliation, he did not cite theories of forgiveness. He referenced twenty-seven years in a prison cell and the choice he made when he walked out of it. The personal narrative gave moral weight to every word that followed. Personal story amplifies authority because it signals something that no qualification or credential can signal lived experience.

This is the difference between someone who knows about struggle and someone who has been inside it. The audience always feels which one is speaking.

The Sensory Detail Principle

Here is an addition that separates adequate storytelling from genuinely immersive storytelling.

The brain does not simulate abstractions. It simulates specifics.

When you say "it was a difficult morning," the listener receives information. When you say "it was six in the morning, still dark, and the auto-rickshaw driver was arguing on his phone while I sat with a presentation I had not slept to finish," the listener is transported. The sensory details — the darkness, the sound, the physical discomfort — activate the sensory cortex. The listener is no longer hearing about your experience. They are briefly having it.

Train yourself to include at least one sensory anchor in every story you tell. A sound, a temperature, a smell, a physical sensation, a specific visual detail. These are not decorations. They are the mechanism through which a listener enters the scene rather than observing it from outside.

One specific detail does more than three general ones. Choose carefully. Make it real.

The Vulnerability Principle

There is a reason audiences trust certain storytellers completely and remain at a distance from others, even when both are telling true stories.

The difference is vulnerability.

Vulnerability in storytelling does not mean emotional performance or oversharing. It means being honest about the moment when the outcome was uncertain, when you did not know what to do, when you were wrong, when you were afraid. It means allowing the audience to see the struggle rather than only the resolution.

Most speakers skip the struggle. They move quickly from context to lesson, wanting to appear capable and composed. But in doing so, they remove the very element the audience needs to identify with. The audience does not connect with your success. They connect with your doubt, your confusion, your very human moment of not knowing. That is where they find themselves in your story. And finding themselves in your story is the moment influence begins.

Strength without vulnerability is information. Strength with vulnerability is story.

The Invisible Character: Your Listener

Every story has an invisible character that most storytellers forget to include.

The listener.

Powerful storytelling is not a monologue. It is a mirror. The best stories are constructed with the listener's experience in mind — what do they already know, what have they already felt, where in this narrative will they recognise themselves? This is why Zakir Khan's stories work across age groups, cities, and backgrounds. He is not telling his story. He is telling the audience's story through his own experience. His specifics are so precisely chosen that they unlock something universal.

Before you tell any story, ask yourself one question: *where in this story will my listener find themselves?* If you cannot answer that question, the story is not yet ready to be told.

The Emotional Arc and Tension

Every impactful story moves through tension and release. This is not a creative choice. It is a biological necessity.

If tension never rises, the audience disengages. There is nothing at stake, so there is no reason to stay attentive. If release never comes, the audience feels incomplete. The brain has been promised resolution and denied it, which creates frustration rather than impact.

The emotional arc of a story should feel like breathing. Tension builds on the inhale. Release arrives on the exhale. A flat narrative is a story told on a single breath — steady, even, and forgettable. Structured tension is what keeps the listener in the room, leaning forward, waiting to exhale.

Storytelling as an Influence Mechanism

Influence operates on three levels simultaneously when the story is used correctly.

The first is cognitive clarity. Stories make abstract ideas concrete. You can explain the importance of preparation for years, or you can tell a two-minute story about someone who was not prepared and what it cost them. The story does what the explanation could not: it makes the idea visible.

The second is emotional connection. Stories create identification. Once a listener has seen themselves inside your narrative, they are no longer evaluating your argument from a distance. They are inside it with you.

The third is credibility. Personal stories signal authenticity in a way that cited research and borrowed examples never fully can. They say: I have been here. I know this from the inside. That signal builds trust faster than any credential.

When these three levels align, persuasion stops feeling like persuasion. It feels like shared understanding.

The Compression Exercise

Choose a real experience from your own life. Something that changed how you thought, felt, or acted. Then write it across six questions:

Where was I and what was happening around me? What conflict or problem appeared? What did I struggle with internally or externally? What shifted — what changed or what did I realise? How did it resolve? What did I learn, and why does it matter beyond just my own experience?

Now tell it in two minutes. Then compress it to one minute. Then to thirty seconds.

This is not a reduction exercise. It is a clarity exercise. Every compression forces you to identify what is essential and release what is merely background. If you cannot reduce the story, you do not yet fully understand its core. Constraint does not weaken a story. It reveals it.

The Discipline Rule

Never tell a story without purpose. Never end a story without extracting meaning. Never mistake length for depth. The most powerful stories are often the shortest ones — the ones where every sentence has earned its place, where nothing is present for the teller's comfort and everything is present for the listener's experience.

Storytelling is not entertainment. It is structured emotional transmission.

And like every other skill in this book, its power is not in the telling.

It is in the preparation that makes the telling feel effortless.

CHAPTER 12

Applying Storytelling in Real Life

Understanding story structure is one thing. Using it deliberately under pressure, in real conversations, in interviews, meetings, and everyday exchanges, is another.

Most people do not struggle with storytelling because they lack experiences. They struggle because they narrate events instead of building progression. They report what happened instead of constructing meaning from it.

They say: this happened. And then this happened. And then this happened.

That is chronology. Chronology is not a story. The story is causality. And the difference between the two is the difference between being heard and being remembered.

The And Then Problem

The word that kills most stories before they begin is also the most innocent-sounding word in the language.

And then.

And then creates a sequence. Sequence has no tension, no consequence, no forward pull. The listener processes each event in isolation and feels nothing building. By the time the story ends, there is nowhere for the meaning to land.

Compare these two versions of the same experience.

Version one: I joined a team project. And then we had issues. And then I tried to help. And then we finished it.

Version two: I joined a team project, but within the first week it became clear that half the work had not been started. Therefore, I reorganised the responsibilities and introduced daily fifteen-minute check-ins. As a result, we submitted on time and the team leads specifically mentioned the coordination in their feedback.

The facts are identical. The experience of listening is completely different. The second version has tension, action, and resolution. The listener is pulled forward because they sense that something is at stake and they want to know how it resolves.

But creates friction. **Therefore** creates movement. Movement builds engagement.

Train yourself to remove and then from your storytelling vocabulary entirely. Every time you feel the instinct to say and then, ask yourself: is this a but or a therefore? Is this a conflict or a consequence? Answer that question and your story will find its structure automatically.

Storytelling in Interviews

The interview room is where the and then problem causes the most damage, because the stakes are highest and the instinct to simply report is strongest.

When an interviewer asks me about a challenge you faced, the majority of candidates respond with claims rather than stories.

I work well under pressure. I am a strong team player. I handle difficult situations effectively.These are statements. They ask the interviewer to trust them without evidence. And trust without evidence is difficult to give to a stranger across a table.

Stories prove claims. They do not ask for trust. They demonstrate the thing being claimed and allow the interviewer to reach their own conclusion.

Instead of saying I handle pressure well, consider this:

During my final semester, our exam schedule was moved forward by two weeks, but I had already committed to a project deadline that could not be shifted. Therefore I broke my preparation into focused ninety-minute blocks across both commitments and stopped treating them as competing priorities. As a result I submitted the project on time and cleared all my papers. What it taught me was that pressure does not actually create the problem. Unclear prioritization does.

Notice what happened. The claim I handle pressure well was never stated. It was demonstrated. The interviewer saw it rather than heard it. Causality communicates competence in a way that assertion never can.

The reflection at the end is not decoration. It is what separates a capable person from a thinking person. Interviewers remember the lesson more than the event.

The STAR Method — Your Interview Story Framework

In Chapter 11 you learned the architecture of a powerful story: Context, Conflict, Struggle, Shift, Resolution, Lesson. That architecture works beautifully in presentations, personal conversations, and any moment where you have the space to let a story breathe fully.

Job interviews require a compressed version of that architecture. The interviewer is moving through a structured conversation with multiple candidates. They need your story to be complete, specific, and efficient. The STAR Method is the framework built for exactly that context.

STAR stands for Situation, Task, Action, Result.

Situation — Set the scene briefly. Where were you, what was the context, what was happening around the decision or challenge you are about to describe. This should be two to three sentences maximum. Do not spend time here. The situation is the frame, not the story.

Task — What specifically were you responsible for in that situation. What was your role, your challenge, your individual accountability. This is where you establish what was actually at stake for you personally rather than for the organisation in general.

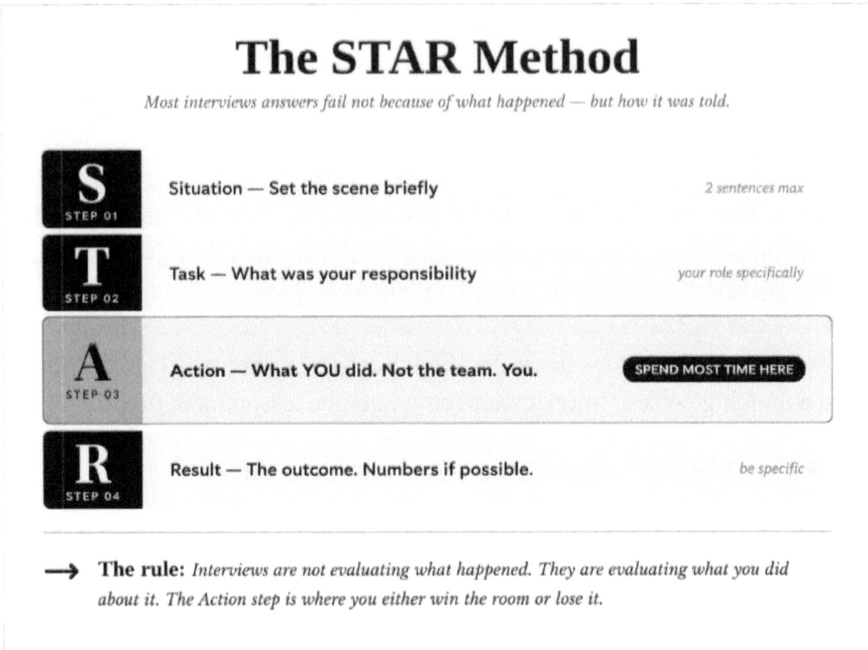

Action — This is the heart of the STAR answer and where most candidates spend too little time. Describe specifically what you did. Not what the team did, not what the process dictated, not what anyone else contributed — what you decided, initiated, and executed. Use the word I deliberately and without apology. Interviews are evaluating you. Own your contribution fully.

Result — What was the outcome of your action. Wherever possible, make this specific and measurable. Not many things improved but customer satisfaction scores rose by eighteen percent over the following quarter. Not the project was a success but we delivered the system three weeks ahead of deadline and fifteen percent under budget. Numbers are not essential if genuine numbers do not exist — but specificity always is.

Here is a complete example of a STAR answer to the question: tell me about a time you had to lead through a difficult situation.

Situation: In my second year at my previous organisation, our team lead resigned unexpectedly two weeks before the delivery deadline of a major client project. The team had lost momentum and there was genuine uncertainty about whether the deadline was still achievable.

Task: I was a senior team member at the time, not formally in a leadership role, but I recognised that someone needed to step in and reorganise the remaining work or the deadline would be missed.

Action: I called an informal team meeting that afternoon — not waiting for management to assign a replacement. I mapped out what remained to be delivered, redistributed the tasks based on each person's capacity and strengths, established a daily fifteen-minute check-in so blockers could be resolved quickly, and kept direct communication with the client's project manager so they were never left without information.

Result: We delivered the project on the original deadline. The client extended their contract with us for the following year, and my manager formally recognised the initiative in my performance review. I was promoted to team lead six months later.

Notice what this answer does. It is specific rather than general. It is personal rather than collective. It moves quickly through the situation and task so it can spend the most time on action — which is where the interviewer is learning most about you. And it closes with a result that is concrete and consequential.

The STAR structure is not limited to formal interview settings. Any time you need to demonstrate competence through a specific example — in a performance review, when pitching for a project, when building credibility with a new team or client — STAR gives your story the precision and professionalism that makes it land.

The difference between a candidate who says I am good at handling pressure and a candidate who delivers a complete STAR answer about a specific high-pressure moment is not a difference of personality or experience. It is a difference of preparation and structure. Both may have identical capability. Only one communicates it in a way the interviewer can actually evaluate and remember.

Exercise — Build Your STAR Story Bank

Identify five significant professional experiences from your history — moments of challenge, leadership, problem-solving, failure and recovery, or exceptional delivery. Write a complete STAR answer for each one. Keep each answer between ninety seconds and two minutes when spoken aloud. Practise them until they feel natural rather than rehearsed. These five stories will cover the vast majority of behavioural interview questions you will ever face — because most behavioural questions are asking for the same underlying qualities expressed through different situations.

Storytelling in Professional Settings

In workplaces, most communication defaults to procedural reporting. Updates, summaries, and status checks that sound like this:

We had a delay. And then we contacted the supplier. And then it was resolved.

This is information delivery. It fulfills the minimum requirement of communication without doing anything beyond it. The listener receives the update and forgets it within the hour.

Now restructure the same update using causality:

We faced a two-day delay because of a miscommunication with the supplier, **but** investigating it revealed a gap in our approval process that had been creating slower response times for months. **Therefore** we implemented a centralized tracking system. Response time has already reduced by forty percent and the supplier relationship is now cleaner than it was before the delay happened.

Same situation. A completely different impression. The first version reports a problem that was solved. The second version demonstrates strategic thinking, initiative, and the ability to extract value from difficulty.

Narrative framing does not just make updates more interesting. It positions the speaker as someone who thinks about causes and consequences rather than simply managing events as they arrive. That positioning accumulates. Over time it is what separates people who are seen as executors from people who are seen as leaders.

Micro-Storytelling

Not every story requires five minutes and a room full of people.

Some of the most effective storytelling happens in twenty seconds, in the middle of a conversation, without any formal structure visible to the listener. These are micro-stories — compressed narratives that humanise a point and make it stick without demanding attention.

Here is an example of a micro-story used in a casual professional conversation:

My first client presentation went badly because I focused entirely on the data and forgot the person sitting across the table, but that experience made me rebuild how I prepare entirely. Now I spend as much time thinking about the listener as I do about the content. The results have been different since then.

Three sentences. Clear arc. A conflict, a consequence, a shift, and a lesson — all present, none laboured. The listener receives a complete narrative impression without feeling that a story was being told to them.

Micro-stories are particularly powerful in introductions, in responses to unexpected questions, and in moments where you want to establish credibility without appearing to try. They work because they are specific enough to feel true and brief enough to feel respectful of the listener's time.

One precise micro-story does more for your credibility in a conversation than ten minutes of confident claims.

The VAKS Framework: From Reporting to Reliving

There is a level of storytelling beyond structure, beyond causality, beyond the but and therefore framework. It is the level where the listener stops processing your words and starts experiencing your scene.

Reaching that level requires sensory detail. And sensory detail can be approached systematically through a framework called VAKS — Visual, Auditory, Kinesthetic, and Smell.

The reason this works is neurological. Sensory details do not just add color to a story. They activate specific regions of the brain that process actual sensory experience. When a listener hears a precise visual detail, the visual cortex responds. When they hear a physical sensation described accurately, the sensory areas simulate it. The brain begins to inhabit the scene rather than observe it from outside. And what the brain inhabits, it remembers.

The visual layer is the most accessible. Most storytellers already include some visual detail, but the difference between effective and ineffective visual description is specificity.

Reporting: the hall was crowded. Reliving: rows of white plastic chairs filled every available space and people were standing along the back wall three deep.

The second version creates an image. The listener sees it. The general description asks the listener to imagine something vague. Specific description gives them something precise to inhabit.

The auditory layer is frequently overlooked and disproportionately powerful. Sound creates immediacy. It places the listener inside the moment rather than outside looking in.

Reporting: I was nervous waiting for my result. Reliving: the corridor was quiet enough that I could hear the ceiling fan and the sound of my own breathing.

When Zakir Khan recreates a conversation with his father, he does not summarise the tone. He recreates it — the specific rhythm of the words, the pause before a particular sentence, the quality of the silence that followed. The audience does not just understand that the conversation was tense. They feel the tension in their own chest because the sound of it has been made real.

The kinesthetic layer is where emotional experience becomes physical and therefore undeniable.

Reporting: I felt anxious before the presentation. Reliving: my throat had tightened and there was a specific weight in my chest that made each breath feel slightly shorter than it should have been.

Physical sensation humanises experience in a way that emotional vocabulary cannot. Saying I felt anxious asks the listener to trust your emotional report. Describing the physical sensation invites them to feel it themselves. The difference in impact is significant.

The smell layer is used rarely and for that reason lands with unusual power when it appears. Smell is the sense most directly connected to memory and emotion. A single olfactory detail can transport a listener more completely than a paragraph of visual description.

Reporting: it reminded me of my school days. Reliving: the room smelled of chalk dust and old wooden desks and I was eleven years old again for a moment.

Use this layer sparingly. One smell detail placed at precisely the right moment in a story does more than five visual details spread across the same length. Its power comes from restraint.

Integrating VAKS with Causality

The full form of applied storytelling combines both frameworks — the logical architecture of causality with the sensory immersion of VAKS. When these two operate together, the listener experiences both the logic of what happened and the feeling of being inside it.

Here is what that integration looks like in practice:

The examination hall was silent except for the sound of papers turning, but when the invigilator announced that the paper had been extended by thirty minutes, I felt the tension in the room change completely. Half the students around me exhaled. The other half seemed to tighten. I noticed my own shoulders drop slightly with relief. Therefore, I used that extra time not to rewrite what I had written but to read it as though someone else had written it. What I found surprised me. Three answers that I had been certain about needed significant additions. That experience taught me that certainty and accuracy are not the same thing, and that the most valuable thing you can do with extra time is approach your own work with a stranger's eyes.

Context with sensory detail. Conflict introduced with but. Observation of physical response. Action driven by therefore. Resolution expressed through reflection. Every element present. Nothing unnecessary. This is not a formula to follow mechanically. It is a set of principles to internalise until they become instinct. The goal is not to construct stories consciously while telling them. The goal is to have prepared them well enough that the telling feels natural.

The Three Rules of Real-Life Storytelling

Every story you tell in a professional or academic context should be measured against three standards before it is told.

Relevance. Does this story serve the conversation it is entering? A story told for its own sake, however well-constructed, is self-indulgence. A story told in direct service of the point being made is influence.

Brevity. Have you removed every element that does not increase tension, deepen character, or advance the lesson? Unnecessary background is the most common way strong stories lose their power. The listener does not need to know everything that happened. They need to know everything that matters.

Reflection. Does the story end with meaning extracted, or does it simply end with the final event? Stories without reflection are diaries. They record what happened. Stories with reflection are influential. They show what it means. The reflection does not need to be long. One sentence of genuine insight is more powerful than a paragraph of summary.

Let Me Explain Storytelling Through My Own Story

How LearningNow Podcast Began

One summer vacation, after nearly ten hours of studying throughout the day, I finally went to bed around midnight. It was one of those hot summer nights where electricity becomes more important than you realise. Just as I was about to fall asleep, the power went out. The room became warm and uncomfortable, and sleep disappeared with it.

After some time, the electricity returned. I tried to sleep again, but I couldn't. So I picked up my phone, opened YouTube, and searched for something to listen to. My plan was simple: play a podcast, plug in my earphones, and hopefully fall asleep somewhere in the middle.

But things happened very differently.

I came across a podcast by Nikhil Kamath featuring YouTube CEO Neal Mohan. What was supposed to be background noise quickly became the most interesting thing I had heard all day. Instead of falling asleep, I found myself completely absorbed in the conversation. At one point, Neal Mohan spoke about how YouTube was encouraging the growth of new podcasters and long-form creators.

That single statement planted an idea in my mind.

Before closing my phone, I opened my notes app and typed a single word: **"Podcast shit."** It was not a name or a plan. It was simply a reminder to revisit the idea the next morning.

During that summer vacation, I shared the idea with my sister, Simran Nanda, who would later become the producer of my podcast. She immediately supported it. She believed it would help me grow as a communicator and as a person.

The encouragement felt good, but it did not remove the reality of the situation. I had no experience in podcasting. I had no audience, no equipment, and no certainty that any guest would agree to sit down for a conversation with me. The more I thought about it, the more impossible it seemed. Eventually, I decided to put the idea on hold and reconsider it after returning to college.

When the summer vacation ended, college life quickly took over. Classes, assignments, projects, and daily responsibilities filled my schedule. Yet every few days, the same idea would quietly return. What if I actually started a podcast?

To strengthen my confidence, I discussed the idea with a few friends. They encouraged me to try, but they also raised the same concerns that already existed in my head. How would you get guests? How would you record it? Why would anyone watch it? Once again, the idea moved to the back seat.

A few weeks later, however, the thought returned for the third time.

That was when I realised something important. The idea had survived every objection I had thrown at it. No matter how many reasons I found not to start, the desire to create the podcast kept coming back.

So I made a decision.

I was going to create it.

Not when everything became perfect. Not when I had complete confidence. Not when all the problems disappeared.

I was going to create it anyway.

The moment that decision was made, the real work began. I created a list of potential guests and started learning everything I could about recording, lighting, cameras, audio, editing, colour grading, and production. Every day seemed to introduce a new challenge. Whenever I solved one problem, another appeared immediately after it.

Then came the equipment challenge. Since this was my first episode, I could not justify a large budget. With roughly three thousand rupees, I somehow managed to arrange the minimum equipment necessary for a professional-looking recording.

But equipment solved only one problem.

I still needed a guest.

And I still needed a location.

I approached several people and arranged meetings wherever I could. One conversation in the college canteen led to another introduction, which eventually led to my first confirmed guest. The guest problem was solved, but the location problem remained. With the help of friends and several days of searching, that challenge was eventually resolved as well.

Nearly four months after the night the idea first appeared in my mind, I finally recorded my first podcast episode.

I thought the difficult part was over.

I was wrong.

When the excitement settled and I reviewed the footage, I discovered mistakes everywhere. The video had problems. The audio had problems. My questions needed improvement. My delivery felt awkward. My facial expressions were inconsistent. My body language lacked control. Almost every aspect of the episode revealed something that needed work.

For a moment, it was frustrating.

But it was also one of the most valuable learning experiences I had ever had.

For the first time, I could clearly see the gap between where I was and where I wanted to be.

I edited the episode once.

Then I edited it again.

Then I edited it a third time.

Each version fixed mistakes that I had failed to notice in the previous one. After nearly a month of recording, learning, correcting, and re-correcting, I finally published the episode.

The response was far better than I expected. Friends, teachers, and people who knew me personally reached out with words of encouragement and appreciation. The numbers were not what mattered most. What mattered was that an idea that had existed only in the notes section of my phone had become something real.

Since then, podcasting has become a major part of my life. Every episode continues to bring new challenges. New guests create new situations. New technical problems appear. New communication mistakes reveal themselves. Even after multiple episodes, no recording feels perfect.

And that is exactly what keeps me moving forward.

The name of my podcast is **LearningNow**, and the name carries a responsibility of learning. Every episode challenges me to justify it. Every guest teaches me something. Every mistake reveals a lesson. Every problem forces me to learn a skill I did not have before.

What stays with me most is a simple belief: every unique problem comes carrying multiple possible solutions. The problem arrives first, but the solution is usually waiting nearby for the person willing to search for it.

And perhaps the most important lesson of all is this:

Many people spend years waiting for certainty before they begin. What I learned through podcasting is that certainty usually arrives after action, not before it.

Yes, there will be stressful days.

Yes, there will be moments when you question what you are doing.

Yes, there will be times when the discomfort feels larger than the excitement.

But there is also a unique satisfaction that comes from building something that is truly your own.

A satisfaction that comes from knowing you are living your life instead of simply watching it happen.

<u>You can observe this story followed the story arc</u>

Context: Summer vacation, sleepless night, YouTube podcast.

Conflict: No experience, no audience, no guests, no equipment.

Struggle: Months of hesitation, learning skills, finding guests and location.

Shift: The decision to start regardless of uncertainty.

Resolution: First episode recorded and published.

Lesson: Action creates clarity; problems become teachers.

Notice how the words **but** and **therefore** quietly create movement throughout the story.

BUT introduces tension:

- I wanted to start a podcast, **but** I had no experience.
- The idea excited me, **but** uncertainty held me back.
- I arranged equipment, **but** I still needed a guest and a location.

Every "but" creates friction. Friction creates curiosity. Curiosity keeps the listener engaged.

THEREFORE creates consequence:

- The power cut kept me awake; **therefore**, I opened YouTube.
- The idea remained in my mind; **therefore**, I began researching.
- I committed to the goal; **therefore**, I started solving problems.

"But" creates the obstacle. "Therefore" creates the response. Together, they create narrative momentum.

The story also uses sensory details through the VAKS framework.

Visual: A dark summer night, a glowing phone screen, a college canteen meeting, a recording setup built on a limited budget.

Auditory: A podcast playing through earphones, conversations with friends and family, discussions with potential guests.

Kinesthetic: The discomfort of a hot room during a power cut, the frustration of reviewing mistakes, the excitement of publishing a first episode.

Smell and Atmosphere: The summer environment, the feeling of being awake long after midnight, and the emotional atmosphere surrounding each stage of the journey.

These details help the listener experience the story instead of simply receiving information about it.

That is the ultimate goal of storytelling.

Not to tell people what happened.

To help them feel what happened.

The Rewrite Drill

Take one story you tell regularly — in introductions, in interviews, in casual conversation. Write it out exactly as you currently tell it. Count how many times and then appear.

Now rewrite it. Replace every and then with either but or therefore. Add one visual detail and one physical sensation. End with a single sentence of reflection that could apply beyond your own specific situation.

Read both versions aloud.

The difference will not be subtle. The second version will feel sharper, more intentional, more complete. Not because the experience changed, but because the architecture finally matches the meaning that was always inside it.

Constraint does not limit a story. It reveals it.

The Final Principle

Facts answer questions. Stories shape belief.

Chronology informs. Causality persuades.

Reporting explains. Reliving influences.

If you want to be heard, structure your ideas. If you want to be remembered, structure your experience into tension, consequence, and meaning. If you want to influence — genuinely move someone from where they are to where you want them to be — give them a story they can live inside briefly.

Not because it is more entertaining than argument.

Because it is more human.

And we have always trusted what feels human far more than what merely sounds correct.

PART VII

ADVANCED COMMUNICATION INTELLIGENCE

Clarity makes you understandable. Structure makes you organized. Voice makes you impactful. Story makes you influential. But there is a level beyond all of these that most communication training never reaches.

The speakers and leaders who create lasting influence are not simply the ones who express themselves well. They are the ones who perceive accurately. They read what is not being said as clearly as what is. They respond to what is actually happening in a conversation rather than what they assumed before they walked in. Advanced communication is not about speaking better. It is about perceiving better.

The most powerful communicators are not those who dominate conversations. They are those who listen with genuine attention, read emotional signals beneath the surface of words, and respond with intention rather than reaction. This is where communication becomes intelligence rather than skill. And intelligence cannot be faked under pressure.

In this section we move from expression to perception. Because communication is not complete until the person on the other side feels genuinely understood.

DOES YOUR EMOTION
CLOUD YOUR VISION?

Chapter 13

Emotional Signals and Listening

There is a particular kind of conversation that most people have experienced but few have examined closely.

Someone asks how you are. You say fine. They nod and move on. But you were not fine. And somewhere in the exchange, part of you noticed that they did not notice. The word was correct. Everything beneath it was not. And the person you were speaking to never looked past the word to find out.

This is the gap that separates ordinary communication from intelligent communication. Not vocabulary, not structure, not even delivery. The ability to hear what is actually being said beneath what is being spoken.

Most people listen to respond. Very few listen to understand. And there is an enormous difference between the two.

Two Conversations Happening Simultaneously

Every conversation carries two layers operating at the same time.

The first is the verbal layer — the actual words being used, the content of the message, the information being exchanged. This is the layer most people are trained to attend to.

The second is the emotional layer — the tone beneath the words, the pace of breathing, the posture of the body, the micro-pauses before certain answers, the subtle tightening that appears when a particular topic is introduced. This layer is rarely spoken. But it is always present. And it is almost always more honest than the first.

When someone says it is fine while their shoulders pull slightly inward and their eye contact breaks, the two layers contradict each other. The word says one thing. The body says another. An ordinary listener hears the word and moves on. An intelligent listener notices the mismatch and stays with it.

Most misunderstandings in relationships, workplaces, and conversations do not occur because the wrong words were chosen. They occur because the emotional layer was missed entirely.

The Three Layers of Signal

Reading a conversation accurately requires attention at three levels simultaneously.

Verbal content is what is said. This is the surface. It is the easiest layer to access and the least reliable indicator of what is actually happening internally.

Vocal tone is how it is said. The pace of delivery, the presence or absence of warmth, the slight elevation of pitch under stress, the flatness that appears when someone has stopped caring about the outcome. Emotion leaks through tone before it finds its way into words. A person can control their vocabulary while their voice betrays everything.

Physical cues are how the body behaves while speaking. The signals explored in Chapter 9 — posture, gesture, eye contact, self-touch — do not only apply to the speaker. They apply to everyone in every conversation. When someone becomes physically still in response to a question, that stillness carries information. When someone leans back slightly as a new idea is introduced, the body has registered something the mouth has not yet addressed.

Intelligent listening means attending to all three layers simultaneously and noticing when they align and when they contradict. The contradiction is always where the real conversation is waiting.

Patterns Reveal More Than Moments

A single signal in isolation can be misleading. A pattern of signals across a conversation tells a story that is much harder to misread.

If someone becomes quieter every time a particular topic arises, that topic carries emotional weight they are not ready to express directly. If someone's responses become shorter and more clipped as a conversation continues, something in the exchange is creating discomfort. If someone who has been speaking freely suddenly begins choosing words with visible care, they have entered territory that feels risky to them.

The goal is not to analyse people clinically or to turn every conversation into an exercise in psychological observation. The goal is to be present enough that you notice what is actually happening rather than only what is being said. Most people are so focused on formulating their next response that they stop receiving what the other person is transmitting. Listening intelligently requires suspending the preparation of your reply long enough to fully absorb what is in front of you.

What you hear when you do this changes the quality of everything you say next.

The Half of Communication Nobody Practises

Every communication course ever designed spends the majority of its time on speaking. How to structure your words. How to use your voice. How to present, persuade, and perform. Speaking is visible. Speaking is measurable. Speaking feels like the active half of communication and, therefore, the half worth training.

Listening is treated as the passive half. The waiting half. The part that happens automatically while the other person speaks.

This is one of the most consequential misunderstandings in all of human communication.

Listening is not passive. It is not automatic. And it is not half that happens while you wait for your turn. It is an active, skilled, trainable capacity — and in most real-world communication situations, it is more powerful than anything you could say.

Here is why.

When you speak, you transmit. You put something into the room. But transmission alone does not create connection, trust, or understanding. Every salesperson who has ever talked a customer out of a decision they were already ready to make knows this. Every manager who has ever delivered a perfectly structured piece of feedback and watched the team member shut down knows this. Every person who has ever ended a difficult conversation feeling more misunderstood than when it began knows this.

Speaking without listening is a monologue wearing the costume of a conversation. The people who are described as extraordinary communicators — the ones others seek out, trust instinctively, and feel genuinely understood by — are seldom the most impressive speakers in the room. They are the most attentive listeners. They make the person speaking to them feel like the most important person in the space. They do not just hear the words. They receive the person behind the words.

That quality — genuine, skilled, present listening — is rarer than eloquence. It is more valued than fluency. And it is built not by waiting quietly while others speak but by learning to listen at levels most people never reach.

Reflective Listening

The most powerful tool available to an intelligent listener is also the simplest and the least used.

Reflection.

Reflective listening means returning to the speaker an accurate summary of what you understood them to say, including the emotional content, not just the factual content. It sounds like this:

It sounds like that situation left you feeling overlooked rather than just frustrated by the outcome.

Or: what I am hearing is that it was not the decision itself that hurt but the fact that no one consulted you before it was made.

Reflection does several things simultaneously. It confirms to the speaker that they have been genuinely heard. It allows them to correct any misunderstanding before the conversation continues. And it slows the exchange down to a pace where real understanding becomes possible rather than assumed.

People calm down when they feel understood. Not when they feel agreed with. Not when they feel fixed. When they feel understood. That distinction matters more in communication than most people realize. An agreement can be given without understanding. Understanding cannot be faked. The speaker always knows the difference.

The Discipline of Not Solving Immediately

There is a reflex that many communicators, particularly those who are capable and well-intentioned, struggle to override.

The reflex to fix.

The moment a problem is presented, the mind moves immediately toward a solution. An answer is prepared. Advice is offered. A path forward is suggested. And the person sitting across the table, who came not for a solution but for acknowledgement, feels subtly dismissed. Their experience was converted into a problem to be solved before it had been fully felt.

Emotional intelligence in communication requires the ability to stay in the discomfort of someone else's difficulty long enough to acknowledge it before attempting to resolve it. This is harder than it sounds because sitting with someone else's pain without immediately trying to remove it feels, from the inside, like failing them. It is not. It is respecting them.

Before offering solutions, ask one question: do you want advice right now, or do you need me to listen?

That single question has ended more arguments, repaired more relationships, and prevented more misunderstandings than most communication techniques combined. It signals that you understand the difference between the two needs. And it gives the other person the rare experience of being asked what they actually need rather than having it assumed.

Long before I understood the theory behind listening, I had already seen its effects.

As a teacher, students would often approach me with questions that they hesitated to ask elsewhere. Some questions were thoughtful. Some were basic. Some were questions they worried might sound silly. Yet they still came and asked.

One student once told me, One student once told me, "Sir, you're different. We don't hesitate to ask you any type of questions."At first, I assumed the reason was knowledge.

Later, I realised it was something else.

Whenever a student asked a question, I listened to it with the same curiosity they had while asking it. I did not dismiss a question because it was simple. I did not rush them because I already knew the answer. Whether the question was advanced or basic, I treated it as worthy of attention.

Without realising it, I had already learned one part of listening.

But I had not yet learned the most important part.

For a long time, whenever friends came to me with problems, I immediately moved into solution mode. Before they had finished speaking, I would already be analysing the situation and preparing advice. I genuinely wanted to help, so I assumed that helping meant solving.

Then one conversation changed the way I thought about it.

A close friend came to me carrying a problem that had been weighing heavily on him. As he explained the situation, I did what I had always done. I started offering suggestions, perspectives, and possible solutions. The more he spoke, the more advice I gave.

At one point, he became emotional and even started crying while describing what he had been going through.

Yet I continued trying to solve the problem.

Looking back, I can see that the conversation slowly moved away from emotional support and toward a debate about solutions. I was trying to fix the situation while he was trying to express what he was feeling.

Neither of us realised it at the time.

The conversation eventually ended, but something about it stayed with me.

Later, I began reflecting on what had happened. I realised that although my intentions were good, I had spent most of the conversation listening for problems instead of listening for emotions. I was hearing the facts but missing the experience behind them.

That realization changed the way I approached conversations.

I started experimenting with something different. Instead of rushing toward solutions, I listened longer. I allowed people to finish their thoughts completely. I asked more questions. I became comfortable with silence. And whenever possible, I waited before offering advice.

The results surprised me.

People opened up more. Conversations became deeper. Friends often seemed calmer and clearer before I had offered a single suggestion. In many cases, they did not need an answer as much as they needed a space where they could think aloud without interruption.

That was when I finally understood something I had missed for years.

People do not always come to us because they need solutions.

Sometimes they come because they need understanding.

And understanding begins long before advice does.

It begins with listening.

Listening as Influence

Here is the paradox that most people miss entirely.

The communicators who are trusted most deeply are not the ones who speak most powerfully. They are the ones who listen most completely.

When someone feels genuinely heard, something shifts in them. The defensiveness relaxes. The guardedness reduces. The emotional space that was occupied by the need to be understood becomes available for something new. And in that space, the listener who waited, who reflected, who stayed present without rushing to speak, now carries an influence that no amount of eloquent argument could have created.

Trust earned through listening is a different quality of trust than trust earned through impressive speech. It is deeper, more durable, and more transferable. It says: " This person sees me accurately. And we will follow people who see us accurately far further than people who merely impress us.

Listening is not the passive half of communication. It is strategic empathy. And it is, for most people, the single highest-leverage communication skill they are not yet developing.

Chapter 14

Communication and Love Languages

Advanced communication does not end at the boundary of professional life.

It extends into every relationship you carry. The way you speak to a parent, a partner, a colleague, a friend. The way you express care, appreciation, and acknowledgment. And more importantly, whether the way you express these things is actually being received in the way you intend.

Most people assume that if they care, the other person will feel it. This assumption is responsible for more relational damage than almost any other single misunderstanding in human communication.

Caring is not the same as communicating care effectively. And the gap between the two is where most relationships quietly deteriorate.

The Framework

In 1992, American author and counsellor Gary Chapman published a book that would go on to sell over twenty million copies across the world. The Five Love Languages proposed something immediately recognisable to almost everyone who read it: people do not all experience love, appreciation, and care through the same channel. What makes one person feel deeply valued leaves another person feeling nothing. What communicates warmth and attention in one relationship creates confusion in another.

Chapman identified five primary channels through which people give and receive emotional connection.

Words of affirmation. Quality time. Acts of service. Receiving gifts. Physical touch.

Understanding these channels does not only transform romantic relationships. It transforms professional ones, family dynamics, friendships, and any situation where you need another person to feel genuinely valued rather than just theoretically appreciated.

Speaking Only Your Language

The most common relational communication failure is not hostility or neglect. It is a mismatch.

A person who values acts of service expresses love by doing things — cooking without being asked, solving problems quietly, handling responsibilities the other person did not request help with. They feel cared for when others do the same for them. But if their partner's primary language is words of affirmation, all of that action arrives in a language they do not fully speak. They notice the effort. But they do not feel the love embedded in it, because love, for them, lives in spoken acknowledgement.

Both people are trying. Both people genuinely care. Neither person feels it the way they need to.

This is not a failure of love. It is a failure of translation.

Advanced communication requires the willingness to express care in the language the other person actually receives, not only in the language that feels natural to you. This is not inauthenticity. It is the highest form of relational intelligence. You are not changing who you are. You are expanding the vocabulary through which you express it.

The Five Love Languages

Words of affirmation are verbal expressions of appreciation, acknowled- gment, and encouragement. For people whose primary language is words, specific and genuine praise carries enormous emotional weight. Saying you handled that with real skill means something different to them than it does to someone else. It does not just describe performance. It lands as care.

Silence, dismissiveness, or consistent criticism does not just feel unhelpful to this person. It feels like rejection. Words, for them, are not decoration. They are emotional currency.

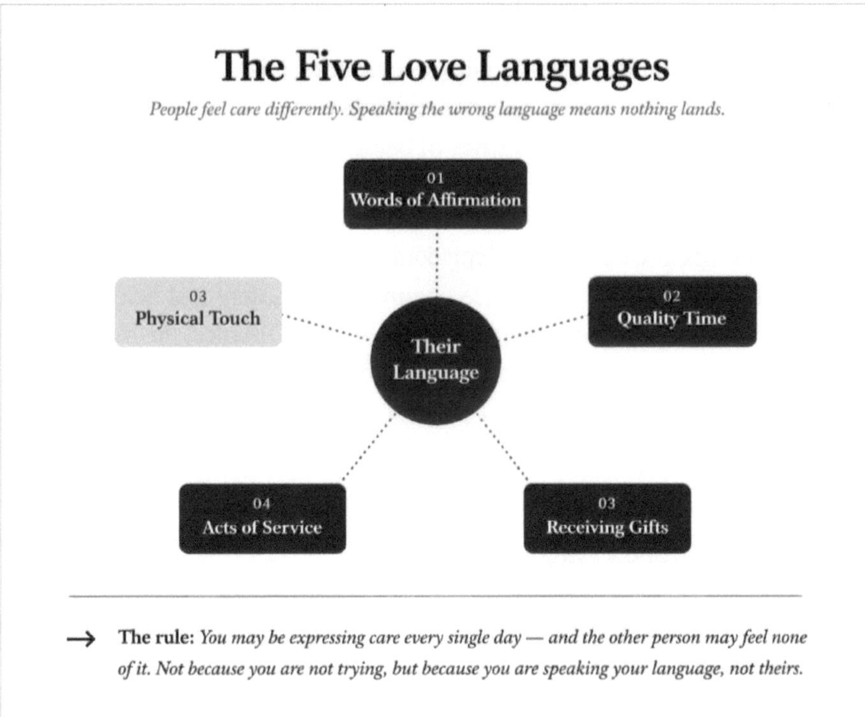

Quality time is an undivided, genuine presence. Not physical proximity while distracted, but actual attentive engagement. Meaningful conversation, shared experience, the feeling of being someone's complete priority for a defined period of time. For people whose primary language is quality time, a cancelled plan or a phone placed on the table between them communicates something specific: you are not my priority right now. The message is rarely intended. It is consistently received.

Acts of service are actions that reduce burden and demonstrate thoughtfulness. Doing something before being asked. Handling a responsibility without making it visible. Anticipating a need and quietly meeting it. For people who speak this language, promises that are not kept are not minor oversights. They are significant withdrawals from an emotional account.

Receiving gifts is frequently misunderstood as materialism. It is not. It is symbolism. A small, thoughtful gift communicates something specific: I was thinking about you when you were not present. I remembered what matters to you. I paid attention. For people who receive love this way, the value of the gesture is not in the object but in the evidence of attention it represents. Forgotten occasions feel like evidence of being forgotten entirely.

Physical touch is an appropriate physical connection — a hug, a hand on the shoulder, sitting close during a difficult conversation. For people whose primary language is touch, physical presence communicates safety and belonging in a way that words and actions alone cannot reach. Distance, in moments of emotional difficulty, can feel like abandonment even when that is the furthest thing from the truth.

Identifying Someone's Language

There are two reliable ways to identify the primary love language of someone important to you.

The first is to observe what they ask for most frequently. People tend to request what they need. Someone who consistently suggests spending time together is telling you something. Someone who notices and mentions acts of service is telling you something. The requests are a map.

The second is to notice what causes the most pain. Pain reveals priority. If being interrupted consistently causes visible distress, words and attention matter deeply. If forgotten plans create disproportionate hurt, quality time is the primary channel. What wounds most clearly identifies what is most valued.

Chapman's framework also suggests a third method: ask directly. This is underused because it feels less romantic or less natural than intuiting. But direct communication — what makes you feel most appreciated, what hurts most when it is absent — prevents years of well-intentioned mismatch and replaces assumption with understanding.

Application

Choose one person whose relationship matters to you. Apply the two observation methods. Form a hypothesis about their primary language. Then, for the next seven days, communicate care deliberately through that channel rather than your own.

Notice what changes.

Not because you have discovered a manipulation technique, but because you have finally begun speaking in a language the other person can actually hear. The care was always there. The translation is what was missing.

The Final Principle

Advanced communication is not about speaking more powerfully.

It is about perceiving more accurately and responding more intentionally.

When you can read the emotional signals beneath spoken words, when you can listen with enough presence to make another person feel genuinely understood, and when you can express care in the language that actually reaches the person you are trying to reach, communication stops being an exchange of information.

It becomes a connection.

And connection, built on accurate perception and intentional expression, is the foundation of every lasting influence you will ever have.

WHAT CONNECTIONS
ARE YOU MISSING?

Chapter 15: The 24 Most Asked Questions About Communication Skills

Every learner, at some point, stops reading theory and starts asking real questions. The kind that comes from actual situations — a conversation that went wrong, a presentation that fell flat, a room that stopped listening halfway through. This chapter collects the most commonly asked questions about communication and answers each one with the depth it deserves. Some answers include frameworks. Some include stories. Some include both. Read it in order or return to specific questions as life demands them. Either way, treat this chapter as a reference you come back to — not something you read once and set aside.

---

1. How do I speak in a way that makes people actually listen to me?

Think about why you stop listening to bad music. It is never the lyrics alone. It is the way the instrument is being played. When a musician cannot hold a note, when the rhythm is unstable, when the sound itself is uncomfortable — you switch off. Not because the song has nothing to say, but because the delivery makes it impossible to stay with.

Your voice is an instrument. And like any instrument, it can be played poorly or played beautifully. When someone speaks in a flat monotone, rushing through ideas without variation or pause, the listener's brain begins to disengage within seconds. Not because the content is weak — but because the instrument is not being played in a way that holds attention.

The question most people ask is how do I get people to listen to what I say. The better question is how do I make the way I say it worth listening to. Those are different problems with different solutions. The first is about content. The second is about delivery. And delivery — pace, pitch, pause, resonance, energy — is entirely trainable. When you learn to play your instrument with intention, people do not just hear you. They stay with you.

---

2. How do I actually become a better communicator?

Through self-awareness. Not the vague, general kind that comes from thinking about yourself, but the specific, confronting kind that comes from observing yourself objectively.

Here is the method. Record yourself speaking for five minutes on any topic. Then review the recording three separate times, each time with a different focus.

The first time, turn the screen away from you and only listen. Close your eyes if it helps. Focus entirely on the sound. What is distracting about your voice? Is the pace too fast? Does the pitch stay flat throughout? Do filler words appear so frequently that they create a rhythm of their own?

The second time, mute the audio entirely and only watch. Observe your body as though you are watching a stranger. What are you doing physically that pulls focus away from your message? Are your hands searching for somewhere to go? Does your posture collapse mid-sentence? Does your face contradict what you are saying?

The third time, get the audio transcribed — using any free transcription tool — and read it on the page. When you see your spoken words in text, patterns that felt harmless in the moment become impossible to ignore. The repeated phrases. The incomplete sentences. The filler words scattered through every paragraph like punctuation that means nothing.

This three-part audit, done honestly and without self-judgment, reveals more about your current communication habits than any course or book can tell you from the outside. You cannot improve what you cannot see. This process makes the invisible visible.

---

3. How do I get better at public speaking and presentations?

Consider how you learned to ride a bicycle. No one handed you a book about cycling and expected you to understand balance from the description. You got on the bicycle, you fell, you got back on, and over time your body learned what your mind could not have taught it. The skill was built through repetition, not understanding.

Public speaking works identically. If you are poor at it, the honest question is not how do I get better — it is how many times have I actually done it? Most people who consider themselves bad at public speaking have barely spoken publicly at all. They have avoided it precisely because they are poor at it, which ensures they remain poor at it indefinitely.

And here is something that changes the entire frame: you do not need a formal stage to practise. When you raise your hand in a team meeting of ten people and share a thought, that is public speaking. When you make a toast at a dinner table, that is public speaking. When you explain something to a colleague in a corridor, that is public speaking. Every single one of these moments is a repetition. Every repetition builds the skill incrementally.

Stop waiting for the right opportunity and start treating every speaking moment as the opportunity. The skill follows volume of practice more reliably than anything else.

The Interview as a Communication Event

One of the highest-stakes public speaking moments most people will ever face is also the one they prepare for least effectively — the job interview.

Most candidates prepare for interviews the wrong way. They prepare for questions. They should be preparing for a conversation.

An interview is not an examination where correct answers earn marks. It is a communication event where the interviewer is trying to answer one question above all others — do I want to spend time with this person? Everything else — qualifications, experience, technical knowledge — is secondary to that single human assessment. And that assessment is made largely through communication, not content.

Here is what that means practically.

Before You Sit Down

The interview begins before you enter the room. Every person you interact with from the moment you arrive — the receptionist, the person who offers you water, the colleague who walks you to the waiting area — is part of the environment you are being observed in. Not formally. Not with a clipboard. But humans assess other humans continuously and unconsciously, and first impressions form in seconds and resist revision stubbornly.

Walk in with your shoulders back and your head level. Not performing confidence — simply not performing anxiety. Greet every person you encounter with genuine warmth. Sit in the waiting area as though you belong there. When you enter the interview room, do not rush to sit. Make eye contact. Offer a firm handshake if the interviewer extends their hand first. Let them direct you to your seat. These small moments of composure communicate more about how you handle pressure than your answer to any question that follows.

The First 90 Seconds

Research on interview psychology consistently shows that most interviewers form a strong initial impression within the first 90 seconds — and spend the rest of the interview unconsciously confirming it.

This means your opening matters enormously.

When you are asked to introduce yourself — and you will be — do not summarise your resume. They have read it. What they have not read is your story. Why this field. Why this role. What drives you beyond the job description. A 60 to 90 second answer that connects your genuine interest to the specific opportunity in front of you does more work than five minutes of credential recitation.

Structure it simply. Where you started. What shaped your direction. Where you are now and why this role is the logical next step. Practise it until it sounds like a conversation, not a performance.

Handling Difficult Questions

Three types of questions unsettle most candidates. Here is how to handle each.

The question you do not know the answer to. Do not pretend. Do not fill the silence with noise while you stall. Say honestly — that is not something I have encountered directly, but here is how I would think through it. Then think through it aloud. What the interviewer learns from watching you reason through an unfamiliar problem is far more valuable than a rehearsed answer to a familiar one.

The question about your weakness. This question is not a trap. It is an assessment of self-awareness. The candidate who says my biggest weakness is that I work too hard has just told the interviewer they lack the self-awareness to answer honestly. Choose a real limitation — one you are genuinely working on — and describe specifically what you are doing about it. Self-awareness combined with agency is one of the most attractive professional qualities available.

The silence after your answer. Many interviewers use deliberate silence after a candidate finish speaking. They wait. They say nothing. And the candidate, uncomfortable, begins filling the silence — walking back their answer, adding unnecessary qualifications, undermining what they just said well. Do not fill that silence. You have answered. Let it stand. A candidate who is comfortable with silence after delivering a strong answer communicates confidence in a way that no additional words can replicate.

Your Questions for Them

Every interview ends with some version of — do you have any questions for us?

This is not a formality. It is the last impression you leave. The candidate who says no, I think you have covered everything has just communicated a lack of genuine curiosity. The candidate who asks one sharp, well-considered question — something that could only come from someone who has thought carefully about this specific opportunity — leaves a distinctly different impression.

Prepare two questions minimum. Not questions about salary or holidays. Questions about the direction of the team, the biggest challenge the role is currently navigating, what success looks like in the first ninety days. These signal that you are already thinking like someone who belongs in the role.

After the Interview

Send a follow-up message within 24 hours. Three to four sentences. Thank them for their time. Reference one specific thing from the conversation that genuinely stayed with you. Restate briefly why you are excited about the opportunity. Most candidates do not do this. Which means the ones who do are remembered.

The single thing that separates interview-ready communicators from everyone else is this — they have practised the conversation aloud, not just in their head. Thinking through your answers is not preparation. Speaking them, hearing them, adjusting them — that is preparation. Your mouth needs the rehearsal, not just your mind.

The Interview Communication Framework

Interviews are not exams. They are communication events.

01 BEFORE YOU SIT DOWN
Presence

- Shoulders back, head level
- Greet every person with warmth
- Sit in the waiting area as though you belong there
- Composure communicates more than words

02 FIRST 90 SECONDS
First Impression

- Introduce your story, not your resume
- Why this field?
- Why this role?
- 60–90 seconds that connect your journey to this opportunity

03 DIFFICULT QUESTIONS

DON'T KNOW	WEAKNESS	SILENCE
Be honest. Say you don't know, then think through it aloud.	Share a real limitation and what you are doing to improve it.	After your answer, pause. Don't fill the silence. Let it stand.

04 YOUR QUESTIONS
Show Curiosity

- Ask thoughtful, specific questions
- Team direction
- Current challenges
- Success in the first 90 days
- Leave a strong last impression

05 AFTER THE INTERVIEW
Follow-Up

- Send a follow-up within 24 hours
- Mention something specific from the conversation
- Reaffirm your interest
- Most candidates don't do this. Be remembered.

THE RULE:
Interviewers are not evaluating how much you know.
They are evaluating what it feels like to communicate with you.

4. How do I listen more effectively?

Most people listen with the intention of responding. While the other person is still speaking, they are already formulating what they are about to say. This means they are only partially present for what is actually being said — and the person speaking almost always senses it, even if they cannot name it.

Genuine listening requires a different orientation entirely. Instead of listening to respond, listen to understand. And then demonstrate that understanding by reflecting back what you heard — not just the content, but the emotion beneath it.

This sounds like: what I am hearing is that you felt overlooked rather than simply frustrated by the decision. Or: it sounds like the timing hurt more than the outcome itself.

When you reflect back accurately, something shifts in the speaker. The defensiveness softens. The need to be heard — which was driving much of the emotional intensity — begins to be met. People calm down not when they feel agreed with, but when they feel genuinely understood. Reflective listening delivers that experience consistently, and it builds a quality of trust in relationships that no amount of clever conversation can replicate.

5. How do I have difficult conversations, including giving negative feedback?

There is a young manager — call him Aryan — who had to tell one of his team members that their work quality had been consistently below what the role required. He had avoided the conversation for six weeks. Every week the avoidance cost more: the team member continued in the wrong direction, the problem compounded, and Aryan's own anxiety about the conversation grew.

When he finally had it, he followed no structure. He called the team member into the room, said he needed to talk about performance, and listed the problems one after another. The team member became defensive immediately. The conversation deteriorated within minutes. Nothing changed. The relationship was damaged.

There is a structure that prevents this outcome. It works consistently across every difficult conversation when applied with genuine care rather than as a script.

First, never have a conversation in a public space. Always take the person aside privately. Public criticism creates shame, and shame closes people down rather than opening them to change.

Second, begin with something genuine and positive. Not flattery — something real. When the other person feels that you see their strengths before you address their weaknesses, they are far more able to receive what follows.

Third, ask for permission before sharing your feedback. Something like: do you mind if I share a few thoughts on how we might improve this going forward? That single question shifts the dynamic entirely. They are no longer receiving a verdict. They are entering a conversation they have agreed to.

Fourth, frame the feedback as a growth opportunity focused on the future rather than a judgment of the past. Fifth, deliver it with warmth and specificity — not I think your work has been poor, but here is a specific area where I think a small change would make a significant difference. Sixth, close on something positive. End where you began — with genuine acknowledgment.

Done this way, difficult conversations become the most powerful tool available for building trust rather than destroying it.

---

6. How do I develop executive presence?

Executive presence is often described as though it is something you either have or you do not. This is incorrect. It is a set of observable, learnable behaviours — and the largest component of it is physical.

Understanding the foundational hand gestures is a practical starting point. There are four worth knowing specifically.

The first is the open palm facing upward. This gesture is warm and inviting. It signals that you are offering an idea rather than imposing one. It reduces perceived threat and increases receptivity in the listener. It is excellent for explaining and sharing. But used exclusively it can lack authority.

The second is the palm facing downward, steady and horizontal. This communicates control, stability, and finality. It signals that you have reached a conclusion and are presenting it with confidence. It is the gesture of someone who is not asking for permission.

The third is the directed point, used very sparingly. A single finger extended toward a point or a person drives authority home with force. Use it at moments of particular emphasis. Use it too often and it reads as accusatory.

The fourth is what can be called the processing gesture — fingertips brought together in front of you, palms apart, in a shape resembling a steeple. This signals thoughtful evaluation. When you are listening to someone and you move into this position, you communicate that you are genuinely considering what they are saying. It projects confidence and intellectual engagement simultaneously.

Moving between these gestures deliberately and intentionally — rather than defaulting to whatever your hands do when you are anxious — is one of the most immediately effective ways to change how you are perceived in any professional room.

---

7. How do I persuade and influence people?

A common misconception about influence is that it lives primarily in what you say — the argument you make, the logic you present, the evidence you provide. In reality, influence operates across four dimensions simultaneously, and verbal content is only one of them.

The first dimension is how people think. Clear, structured communication organises the listener's thinking and makes your perspective easier to adopt as their own.

The second is how people feel. Emotion is not a shortcut around logic — it is what makes logic matter personally. When someone feels something because of what you said, they remember it and act on it differently than when they simply understood it intellectually.

The third is how people behave. This requires the kind of influence that goes beyond a single conversation — it requires consistency, credibility, and trust built over time.

The fourth is what people believe. This is the deepest level, and it is almost exclusively accessed through storytelling. Beliefs do not change through argument. They change through narrative — through experiencing a story that makes a different belief feel true.

Four skills develop influence across all four dimensions: vocal mastery, which controls how your delivery is received emotionally; body language, which shapes perception before words are processed; storytelling, which is where beliefs actually shift; and active listening, which creates the trust that makes all other influence possible. Develop all four consistently and they reinforce each other in ways that make your communication greater than the sum of its parts.

---

8. How do I express my thoughts clearly when speaking impromptu?

There is a particular kind of internal experience that most people recognise. Someone asks you a question unexpectedly. Your mind activates immediately — multiple thoughts arriving at once, none of them fully formed, all competing to be spoken first. And so you speak them all, simultaneously, in whatever order they arrive, and what comes out is a reflection of the chaos inside rather than the knowledge you actually possess.

The listener does not experience your knowledge. They experience your chaos. And they interpret it accordingly.

What separates clear impromptu speakers from scattered ones is not faster thinking or better vocabulary. It is the use of a structure — a framework that gives your thinking a shape before it leaves your mouth. When you begin your answer with the words: there are three aspects to this — your brain immediately begins organising rather than broadcasting. The structure arrives before the content and pulls the content into order behind it.

Frameworks like Problem, Cause, Solution or the PARA method from Chapter 4 are not constraining. They are liberating. They do not limit what you can say. They give what you say somewhere to go.

---

9. How do I develop emotional intelligence in communication?

Consider two managers giving feedback to the same struggling team member. The first manager presents the data clearly and logically. Performance metrics are down. Deadlines are being missed. Here is what needs to change.

Everything said is accurate. Nothing said is wrong.

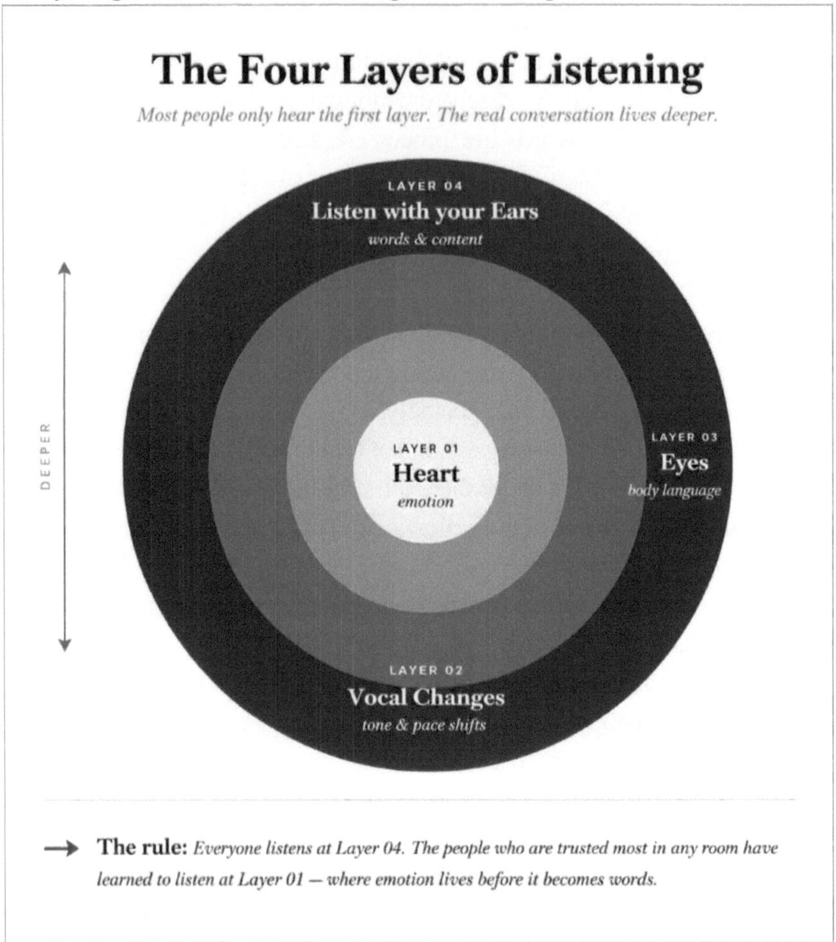

The team member leaves the meeting feeling assessed rather than supported. Within a week they begin quietly looking for other positions.

The second manager begins differently. Before presenting any data, she says: I want to check in with you first. I have noticed something seems different lately and I want to understand what you are experiencing before we talk about anything else.

The team member, who has been managing a family crisis that no one at work knows about, exhales. Tells her. The conversation that follows is completely different — practical, collaborative, and genuinely useful. Three months later the performance has recovered entirely.

The difference between these two managers is not intelligence or competence. It is the ability to listen at a level deeper than words.

Emotional intelligence in communication develops through learning to listen in four specific ways. With your ears — to the content and the words, which most people already do. With your heart — to the mood and emotion beneath the words. When you sense someone is frustrated or anxious, reflect it back: what I am sensing is that you are feeling overwhelmed by this — am I reading that correctly? Even when you are wrong, the act of trying sharpens your ability to read emotion accurately over time. With your eyes — to body language, posture, and the physical signals that appear when someone is uncomfortable or withdrawn. And to vocal changes — the slight quieting, the shorter answers, the flatness that appears when something is wrong but not yet spoken. These four layers together constitute what emotional intelligence actually looks and sounds like in a real conversation.

---

10. How do I tell better stories?

The most common reason stories fail is length. Not lack of drama, not lack of interesting material — length. Most people include two to three times more background than the story actually needs. They begin at the beginning of time rather than at the moment the story actually starts. They include characters who play no role in the tension or the lesson. They explain things the listener could have inferred.

The discipline of storytelling is the discipline of removal. Here is the guiding principle: only tell the story around the peak action, the peak emotion, or the moment the lesson was learned. Everything outside those three zones should be cut without hesitation.

A story about a difficult exam does not need to begin with how you enrolled in the course. It needs to begin the morning of the exam, when you opened the paper and realised the question you had not prepared for was sitting right at the top of the page. That is where the tension lives. Start there. Everything before it is background the listener does not need. Everything after it — the resolution and the lesson — is what they came for.

Precision is not the enemy of a good story. It is what makes a good story powerful.

---

11. How do I become more assertive?

Assertiveness is not volume. It is not aggression. It is the quality of communicating with enough conviction that the listener has no doubt about where you stand — delivered in a way that respects both you and them simultaneously.

Three specific adjustments create it immediately.

End your sentences on a lower pitch. Most people, particularly when nervous or uncertain, allow their sentences to rise at the end — the same pattern as a question. When a statement ends with an upward inflection, it sounds like you are seeking confirmation rather than offering a position. Lower the final note of your sentence and the statement arrives with the authority of someone who means it.

Use grounded, intentional body language. This means gestures that are deliberate and controlled rather than reactive and scattered. It means a posture that stays open and upright rather than contracting under pressure. It means returning to stillness between movements rather than filling every moment with nervous physical noise.

Pause more. This is counterintuitive for people who associate assertiveness with speaking confidently and continuously. But the most assertive communicators are often the ones most comfortable with silence. A pause before answering a difficult question signals that you are not rattled by it. A pause after delivering an important point signals that you stand behind it and are giving it space to land. Confident people are not afraid of silence because they are not trying to fill it with proof that they belong in the conversation.

---

12. What do I talk about with new people?

The anxiety of meeting new people is almost always the anxiety of not knowing how to begin or where to go after the initial exchange. Weather has been discussed. Occupation has been mentioned. And now both people are aware that the conversation has run out of its own momentum.

There is a structure that solves this consistently. It is called High, Low, Buffalo. High is something currently going well for you. Something real, not performed. Low is something you are genuinely finding difficult or challenging right now. Something honest. Buffalo is something interesting or unexpected about you — a hobby, a belief, an experience that most people would not guess.

When you share all three with someone new, you have given them three specific threads to pull on. When they share their three in return, there are six threads in the conversation. Six directions it could go. The pressure of generating topics from nothing disappears entirely because the material is already on the table.

What makes this work is the combination of vulnerability and specificity. The Low creates permission for honesty. The Buffalo creates genuine curiosity.

And genuine curiosity, on both sides of a conversation, is the engine of every connection worth having.

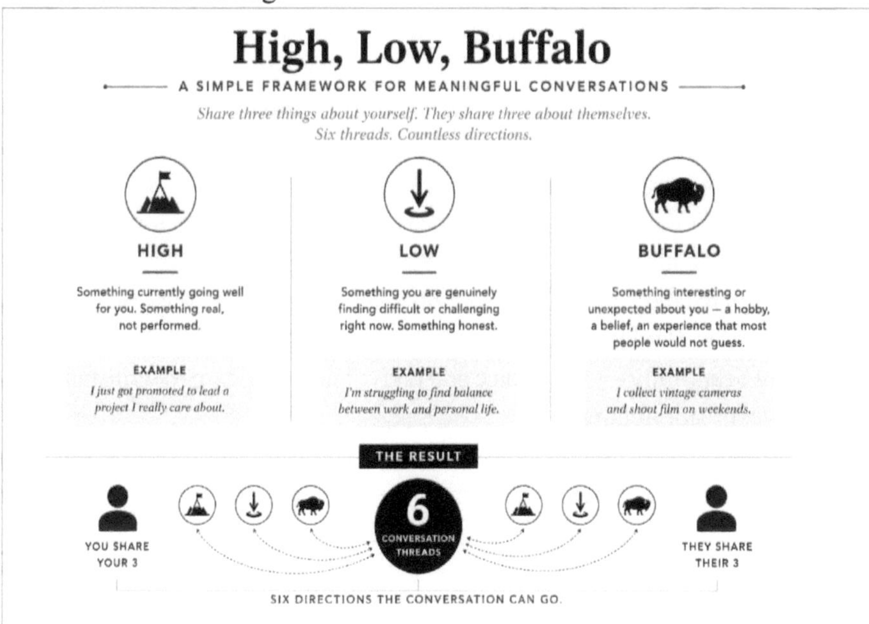

13. How do I overcome the fear of public speaking?

By speaking publicly more often. There is no other answer that is not eventually reducible to this one.

Fear of public speaking is maintained by avoidance. Every time you decline to speak, every time you let the moment pass, the fear receives confirmation that it is protecting you from something genuinely dangerous. And it grows stronger. Every time you speak — however imperfectly, however briefly, in whatever room and to whatever size audience — the fear receives different information. It learns that the situation was survivable. That the audience did not attack. That the worst that happened was a stumble and a recovery. And it loses a small amount of its power.

This is exposure therapy in its most direct form. The only direction that leads to a different outcome is through. Not around. Not away from. Through.

---

14. How do I explain complex ideas simply?

Analogies, metaphors, and similes are the most powerful simplification tools available to any communicator. They work because the human brain learns new things by connecting them to things it already understands. When you provide that connection deliberately, understanding arrives faster and sticks longer than any technical explanation could achieve.

Consider the difference between these two ways of describing the same idea. Vocal mastery involves developing control over rate of speech, tonal variation, the strategic use of pause, volume modulation, and the relationship between breath support and articulation quality. Now consider this: learning to communicate is like learning to play an instrument. First you learn to play the instrument beautifully — your voice and body. Then you learn to write beautiful music — your storytelling.

The information in the second version is less complete. But the understanding it creates is immediately deeper. Because the listener does not need to decode it — they just need to recognise what they already know about music and allow it to illuminate the new concept.

One well-chosen analogy replaces ten minutes of technical explanation and produces better comprehension. This is not dumbing things down. It is respecting the way the human brain actually learns.

---

15. How do I mentor and coach others effectively?

The most effective mentors and coaches share one quality that is rarely discussed in leadership training. They are creative designers of experience rather than effective explainers of information.

There is a fundamental difference between telling someone what they need to learn and creating a situation in which they cannot help but learn it. When a person lives through an experience — when they feel the lesson rather than hear it described — it becomes part of them in a way that no explanation can replicate.

A mentor who wants their mentee to understand the importance of preparation might explain it clearly and compellingly. Or they might put the mentee in a situation where they are underprepared and experience the consequences directly — then debrief the experience afterward. The second approach produces a different quality of understanding. Not intellectual comprehension but embodied knowledge — the kind that changes behaviour rather than just enriching the mind.

The question great coaches ask themselves is not what do I need to tell them but what do I need them to experience? Answering that question honestly and then designing the experience accordingly is what separates good mentors from transformational ones.

---

16. How important is communication to building a personal brand?

Everything you are professionally is communicated through how you communicate. Your expertise, your credibility, your warmth, your confidence, your values — all of these reach the world primarily through the way you speak, write, and present yourself.

Your voice, in the broadest sense of that word, is your personality as others experience it. Not your personality as you experience it internally, but the version of you that other people receive and remember. And that version is almost entirely a function of how you communicate.

This means that levelling up your communication does not just make you a better speaker. It upgrades the entire perception of who you are professionally. The same person, communicating with more clarity, more structure, more presence, and more genuine engagement, will be perceived as more intelligent, more capable, and more worth listening to — without changing a single qualification or experience on their record.

Your personal brand is not built primarily through what you do. It is built through how you communicate what you do.

---

17. How do I make a strong first impression?

A first impression is formed across two channels simultaneously, and most people invest heavily in one while ignoring the other almost entirely.

The first channel is your visual image — how you carry yourself, your posture, your body language, how you dress, and the energy you bring into a room physically. This is the channel most people are aware of and at least somewhat intentional about.

The second channel is your vocal image — the impression people form the moment you open your mouth. The quality of your voice, the pace of your speech, the warmth or flatness of your tone, the confidence or uncertainty in your delivery. This channel is often ignored entirely in preparation for important first impressions, despite the fact that it frequently carries more weight than the visual in the seconds that follow the initial moment of contact.

Attend to both. And if you want to add a third element that most people overlook entirely: how you smell. Scent is processed in the limbic system — the brain's emotional centre — and contributes to first impression and emotional memory more directly than almost any other sensory input. It sounds trivial until you consider how powerfully a particular scent can trigger memory and feeling. Attend to it deliberately.

---

18. How do I get better at receiving feedback?

Consider what happens to someone who consistently reacts defensively when they receive feedback. In the short term, they feel protected. The uncomfortable information is deflected. The criticism does not land.

In the medium term, the people around them stop giving feedback. Not because there is nothing to say — but because the experience of saying it is unrewarding and sometimes unpleasant. The feedback stops. And the person, unaware that this has happened, begins to believe that the absence of feedback means the absence of problems.

In the long term, they stagnate. They do not know their blind spots because no one will tell them anymore. They make the same errors repeatedly without understanding why. Their development slows and eventually stops while people around them, who have actively sought and welcomed honest input, continue to grow.

The people who improve fastest are almost always the people who ask for feedback most frequently and receive it with the most genuine openness. Not because they enjoy criticism — no one does — but because they have trained themselves to filter out the emotional sting and extract the useful signal. Feedback is information. The moment you learn to experience it as data rather than judgment, it becomes one of the most valuable resources available to you.

---

19. How do I respond confidently when put on the spot?

Unexpected questions are among the most anxiety-producing moments in professional communication because they remove the one thing most people rely on most heavily: preparation time.

The framework that resolves this most reliably is called the one thing. When a question arrives without warning, begin your answer with the words: the one thing I would say about that is.

This opening does something specific and immediate. It creates a constraint. You have committed to one point rather than attempting to cover everything your mind is generating simultaneously. That commitment focuses you. And focused communication — even when it covers less ground than scattered communication — is almost always more impactful.

The one thing I would say about the meaning of life is that it is found in the contribution you make to something larger than yourself. That answer is not comprehensive. But it is clear, complete, and delivered with the confidence that comes from knowing exactly where you are going before you begin.

---

20. How do I manage nerves before a speech or presentation?

The nerves themselves are not the problem. As explored in Chapter 5, nervousness is a biological response to perceived exposure — it is adrenaline preparing the body for action. The problem arises when adrenaline has nowhere to go.

When you stand still while adrenaline is circulating, the energy becomes trapped. It appears as shaking hands, an unstable voice, a racing mind, and a pace that accelerates beyond your control. The body is prepared for movement and receiving none.

Give it movement. Star jumps, a brisk walk, push-ups — any form of brief physical activity that allows the adrenaline to discharge through the body rather than remaining trapped in it. After the movement, the nervous system shifts from panic activation to controlled readiness. The nerves do not disappear — a moderate level of activation is actually useful, sharpening focus and adding energy to delivery — but they are no longer in control of you.

Manage the adrenaline through the body. Then speak.

---

21. How do I build genuine confidence in communication?

Learn the skill of improvisation.

Confidence in communication is not primarily built through preparation — though preparation contributes. It is built through the deep, embodied knowledge that you can handle whatever happens. That when the unexpected question arrives, when the technology fails, when the room responds differently than you anticipated, when you lose your thread mid-sentence — you have the internal resources to navigate it.

Improvisation training builds exactly that knowledge. Not because it teaches you to be funny or spontaneous in a performative way, but because it trains you to be genuinely present in a communication moment — to respond to what is actually happening rather than what you planned for. When you know in your body that you can ebb and flow through whatever a conversation or presentation throws at you, confidence stops being something you perform. It becomes something you simply have.

---

22. How do I communicate more authentically?

By exploring the full range of your instrument rather than remaining in the narrow band of expression that habit has assigned you.

Most people, by the time they reach adulthood, have settled into a small portion of their communicative range. The same pace they always use. The same pitch. The same gestures. The same emotional register regardless of what they are actually saying or feeling. This consistency feels natural because it is familiar. But it is not authentic — it is habitual. And there is a significant difference.

Authenticity in communication does not mean saying whatever you feel whenever you feel it. It means having enough range that the full reality of what you are thinking and feeling can actually find expression when the moment calls for it. The more of your instrument you can access, the more of yourself can come through when you speak. That completeness — that sense of a whole person rather than a managed presentation — is what audiences and individuals experience as authentic. And it is built through deliberate exploration of everything your voice and body are capable of.

---

23. When nervous I ramble and speak in circles. What do I do?

The mechanism behind nervous rambling is almost always a combination of two things: shallow breathing and the instinct to fill silence. When anxiety tightens the breath, the mind speeds up to compensate, and speaking becomes the outlet for energy that has nowhere else to go. The words keep coming not because there is more to say but because stopping feels more frightening than continuing.

The intervention is physical, not verbal. Breathe. Not as a vague suggestion but as a specific, deliberate act. A full diaphragmatic breath — slow, complete, felt in the lower ribcage — interrupts the shallow-breathing cycle that is fuelling the rambling. It slows the pace. It gives the mind a moment to find structure. And it signals to the nervous system that the threat level is lower than it believes.

Breathe before answering. Breathe between ideas. Do not be afraid of the pause that breath creates. That pause is not emptiness. It is the moment where scattered speech finds its shape before continuing.

---

24. What is the single most important thing I can do to transform my communication?

Stop being so attached to who you are in the present that you do not give the future version of yourself a chance.

This means something specific and practical. It means being willing to press record and listen back to what you actually sound like rather than what you imagine you sound like. It means staying with that discomfort instead of closing the app. It means practising the pause when everything in you wants to fill the silence. It means using the framework when the habitual ramble feels more natural. It means choosing the structured answer over the comfortable scatter, again and again, until structure becomes the new natural.

The future version of you — the one who speaks with clarity that lands, with a voice that carries authority, with stories that move people, with a presence that the room feels before you say a word — is not a different person. It is you, with different habits.

Those habits are not built through inspiration. They are not built through reading. They are not built through understanding the theory, however clearly it is explained.

They are built through the decision, made quietly and without fanfare, to practise one more time. And then one more time after that.

That decision, repeated consistently across thirty days, across ninety days, across a year — is the only thing that has ever transformed communication from something people struggle with into something they are known for.

The game has rules. You now know them.

Go play.

HOW FAR WILL YOU GO?

PART VIII

THE 30-DAY MASTER PROTOCOL

Before You Begin

Knowledge does not change you. Practice does. Most people believe they already know their communication style. Very few have actually observed it objectively. This protocol exists to close that gap — between what you think you do and what you actually do. The system is simple:

- Record
- Review
- Refine
- Repeat

This framework is inspired by the structured self-audit method taught by communication educator Vinh Giang, built on one foundational principle:

You cannot improve what you do not measure.

Do not skip the diagnosis phase. Improvement without diagnosis is random effort. Random effort produces random results.

Phase One: The Baseline Diagnosis: Complete this phase before Day 1 of the training weeks. It will take approximately one hour and it is the most important hour of the entire protocol.

Step 1: Record a Five-Minute Improvised Video

- Find a quiet space and set your phone to record at eye level
- Speak for five minutes without any preparation or script
- Do not stop, correct yourself, or restart — let it run completely

Why improvised? Because scripts hide habits. Improvisation reveals them. Speak about any of the following:

- Why do you want to improve your communication?
- What do you currently struggle with?
- What is something you believe strongly and why?

This is your baseline — your honest starting point before any training begins. Every improvement across thirty days will be measured against this single recording.

Step 2: create Twenty-Four Hours of Distance

- Do not watch the recording immediately
- Wait a full twenty-four hours before reviewing it
- Return to it as an observer, not a judge

Why distance? When you watch yourself immediately, emotional reaction takes over. Distance replaces self-criticism with objectivity. Mastery requires calm observation. Calm observation requires distance.

Step 3: The Auditory Audit

- Play the recording with the screen facing away
- Listen only — no visual information
- Write down specific observations across these five areas:

1. **Rate of speech** — are you rushing or speaking with controlled pace?
2. **Volume** — too soft, too loud, or inconsistent?
3. **Pitch and melody** — does your voice stay flat or vary with meaning?
4. **Tonality** — does the voice sound warm, tense, uncertain, or engaged?
5. **Pause control** — do you fill every silence or allow deliberate gaps?

Write specific observations. Not *I sound bad* — that is judgment.

Write: *I speak too fast when explaining a new idea. My pitch stays flat regardless of content. I use the word* so *as a filler between every sentence.*

Specific observations can be corrected. Vague ones cannot.

Step 4: The Visual Audit

- Mute the recording entirely
- Watch without sound — observe only the physical layer
- Evaluate and write down observations across these five areas:

1. **Posture and alignment** — does the body stay open and grounded or collapse mid-sentence?
2. **Hand gestures** — do they support your points or create distraction?
3. **Facial expression** — does your face engage with content or remain flat?
4. **Movement patterns** — is there unnecessary shifting, fidgeting, or nervous energy?
5. **Eye contact** — where do your eyes go when thinking or under pressure?

Note both what is working and what is contradicting your message. A person can sound confident while looking hesitant. The visual audit reveals that gap.

Step 5: The Transcription Audit

- Transcribe your recording using any of the following tools:
    - Google Docs voice typing
    - YouTube unlisted upload with auto-captions
    - Otter.ai or Notion AI
    - Manual transcription of key sections for deeper awareness

Once transcribed, go through the text and highlight:

- **Non-words** — um, err, uhh
- **Filler words** — like, so, basically, actually, you know
- **Repeated phrases** appearing more than twice
- **Incomplete sentences** that trail off without landing

- **Vague language** where a specific word would have been stronger

When you see your spoken words on a page, patterns that felt harmless in the moment become impossible to ignore. This is not a reason for discouragement. It is a reason for clarity. You now know exactly what needs to be fixed.

Step 6: Select Your Four Focus Areas

From all three audits, identify your four most significant areas — one from each category:

- **One clarity issue** — filler words, unstructured thinking, incomplete sentences, lack of conclusion
- **One vocal issue** — monotone, rushing, volume inconsistency, weak breath support
- **One presence issue** — collapsed posture, nervous gestures, poor eye contact, excessive movement
- **One storytelling issue** — no tension, missing reflection, no sensory detail, unclear lesson

Only four. Not ten. Not everything. Four.

Focused application creates change. Scattered attention creates the illusion of effort without the result.

The Four-Week Training Structure

The weeks below follow a suggested sequence. However, after completing your audit, you may reorder based on your diagnosis.

- If voice is your most significant weakness — begin with Week 2

- If storytelling is limiting your professional growth — move Week 4 forward
- If presence is your biggest gap — start with Week 3

This is a framework. You own the application of it.

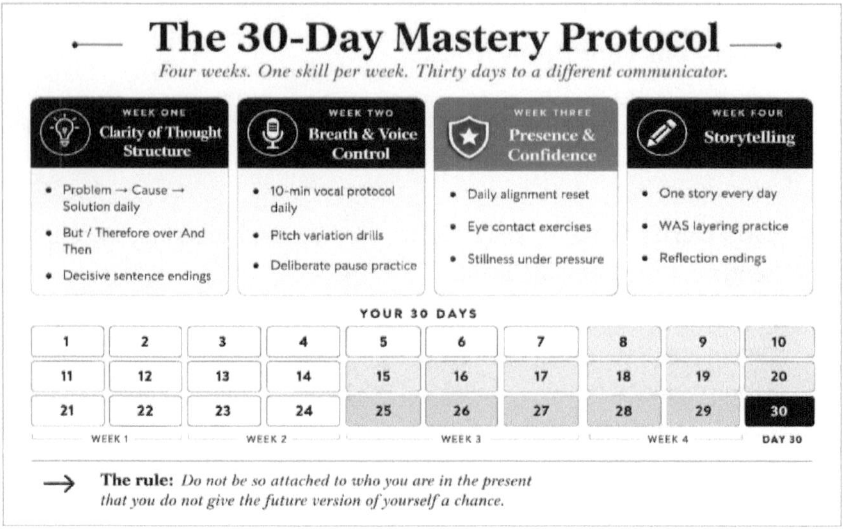

Week One: Clarity and Thought Structure

Focus areas this week:

- Eliminating filler words
- Using structured thinking — 1, 2, 3 points
- Replacing *and then* with *but* and *therefore*
- Ending every sentence with intention — land it, do not trail off

Daily practice:

- Speak one complete idea using three structured points
- Pause deliberately after each point before continuing
- Summarise one conversation or idea each day in under sixty seconds using Problem → Cause → Solution

- Record at least two of these summaries and listen back

What changes this week:

Your thinking begins arriving in order before your mouth opens rather than organising itself while you speak. Clarity reduces mental chaos. Structured thinking lowers anxiety.

Week Two: Breath and Voice Control

Focus areas this week:

- Diaphragmatic breathing before speaking
- Controlled deliberate pausing
- Pitch variation across sentences
- Eliminating monotone stretches

Daily practice:

- Complete the ten-minute vocal conditioning protocol from Chapter 8 every morning:
    - 1 minute humming for resonance
    - 2 minutes lip trills
    - 2 minutes siren pitch slides
    - 2 minutes slow exaggerated tongue twisters
    - 3 minutes structured speaking at full energy
- Read aloud for five minutes with deliberate pitch variation
- Mark the most important word in each sentence and give it noticeably more weight
- Record one two-minute explanation and listen for breath collapse, monotone stretches, and rushed endings

What changes this week:

Your voice begins to feel like something you are directing rather than something that simply happens when you open your mouth.

Week Three: Presence and Confidence

Focus areas this week:

- Posture alignment and the reset technique from Chapter 9
- Power sphere gesture control
- Eye contact discipline
- Reducing nervous movement and returning to neutral

Daily practice:

- Deliver one one-minute explanation standing, using the alignment reset before you begin
- Maintain eye contact with your camera for a full two minutes without looking away
- Between each gesture, return hands to neutral rather than allowing them to search for somewhere to go
- Record one session with sound off and watch only the body — ask: does this person look like they believe what they are saying?

What changes this week:

Your physical presence begins to feel like a choice rather than a reflex. Confidence becomes visible before words are heard.

Week Four: Storytelling and Structured Speaking

Focus areas this week:

- Context → Conflict → Struggle → Shift → Resolution → Lesson
- Using *but* and *therefore* to replace *and then*
- Adding at least one VAKS sensory detail per story
- Ending every story with a reflection that extends beyond personal experience

Daily practice:

- Tell one micro-story every day — keep it under sixty seconds
- Record three of these across the week
- Listen back and ask: did the conflict create genuine tension? Did the ending land with meaning or simply stop? Could a stranger find themselves inside this story?

What changes this week:

You begin building a personal library of structured stories ready to deploy in interviews, presentations, and any moment where influence matters.

Day 30: The Final Recording

- Return to the same setup as Day 1 — same location if possible, same prompt
- Record five minutes, no preparation, no script
- Complete the same three-part audit — auditory, visual, and transcription
- Compare directly with your baseline recording

Look for these specific changes:

- Is the filler word count lower?
- Does the voice vary with meaning?
- Does the body stay grounded through the full five minutes?
- Do sentences conclude with intention?
- Is there a story in there with structure and meaning?

Growth must be visible and measurable.

If you cannot see the difference between Day 1 and Day 30, do not consider the protocol complete. Repeat the cycle with the four focus areas that still need the most work. Mastery is not a destination reached once. It is a standard maintained through continued iteration.

The Philosophy Behind the Protocol

Communication is not identity. It is a habit. The voice you have been using, the pace, the filler words, the posture, the way your thoughts arrive in speech — none of these are who you are. They are patterns formed through repetition over years. And patterns formed through repetition can be reformed through repetition. Vinh Giang closes his communication mastery programme with one line worth carrying beyond this book:

Do not be so attached to who you are in the present that you do not give the future version of you a chance.

The future version of you — the one who speaks with clarity, breathes with control, holds a room with presence, and moves people with story — is not a different person. It is the same person, with better habits. Those habits start with honest observation. And honest observation starts with pressing the record.

Appendix

This section converts awareness into measurement.

If the previous chapters gave you understanding, this section gives you accountability. Understanding without measurement drifts. Measurement without action stalls. This appendix exists to prevent both.

- Use it
- Print it
- Repeat it

Mastery lives here.

---

1. Self-Audit Checklist

Use this checklist during every Record and Review session. Rate yourself honestly from 1 to 5.

1 = Weak 2 = Developing 3 = Consistent 4 = Strong 5 = Automatic

Do not rate how you want to perform. Rate how you actually performed in the recording you just reviewed.

A. Clarity and Structure

- ☐ I speak in clear structured points
- ☐ I avoid rambling and stay on topic
- ☐ I end sentences confidently without trailing off
- ☐ I use but and therefore instead of and then
- ☐ My ideas connect logically from one to the next

Score: / 25

B. Vocal Control

- ☐ My speech pace is controlled and deliberate
- ☐ My volume is appropriate and consistent throughout
- ☐ My pitch has variation and does not stay flat
- ☐ I use pauses intentionally rather than filling them
- ☐ I eliminate filler sounds — um, err, uhh

Score: / 25

C. Physical Presence

- ☐ My posture is aligned and remains upright throughout
- ☐ My gestures stay within the power sphere
- ☐ My hand movements are intentional and return to neutral
- ☐ My eye contact is steady and distributed
- ☐ I avoid nervous fidgeting and unnecessary self-touch

Score: / 25

D. Storytelling Ability

- ☐ I structure stories using Context, Conflict, Shift, and Lesson
- ☐ I use but and therefore to create tension and consequence
- ☐ I include at least one sensory detail to create immersion
- ☐ I end stories with a reflection that carries meaning beyond the event
- ☐ My stories are concise, purposeful, and relevant to the listener

Score: / 25 Total Score: / 100

Repeat this audit every thirty days. Write your score and date each time. Improvement must be visible and measurable. If your score does not move, your practice is not specific enough. Return to the focus area that scored lowest and repeat that week before moving forward.

Score Interpretation

- **80 to 100** — Strong foundation. Focus on refinement and consistency under pressure.
- **60 to 79** — Developing competence. Identify your two lowest sections and prioritise them.
- **40 to 59** — Conscious incompetence. You are aware of the gaps. This is Stage Two from Chapter 2. Stay with the protocol.
- **Below 40** — You are at the beginning. This is not a problem. It is a starting point. Every score above this is progress.

2. Filler Word Tracker

Awareness destroys filler habits. What you can measure, you can reduce.Use this table during every transcription audit. Count each filler word and record the total. Track weekly across the thirty days.

Your goal is not zero. Your goal is reduction.

2. Filler Word Tracker

Awareness destroys filler habits. Track weekly. Your goal is not zero — your goal is reduction.

Date	Umm	Like	So	Basically	You Know	Other	Weekly Total
Week 1							
Week 2							
Week 3							
Week 4							

Replace filler with pause. Silence signals control.

If your Week 1 total is 45 fillers and your Week 4 total is 12 fillers, that is measurable, undeniable growth. The number tells the truth when nothing else will.Every time you feel the instinct to fill silence with a word that carries no meaning, replace it with nothing. A clean pause. Silence signals control. Filler signals avoidance. The tracker makes the difference visible.

3. The 30-Day Progress Sheets

Work on one primary focus per week. Write your focus at the top before the week begins, not after. Commitment before action accelerates growth.Mark each day you complete your practice. At the end of each week, answer the three reflection questions honestly. These answers are not for performance. They are for you.

Week 1

Weekly Focus:

Daily Practice Completed

- Mon ☐ Tue ☐ Wed ☐ Thu ☐ Fri ☐ Sat ☐ Sun ☐

End of Week Reflection

- What improved this week?

- What still feels weak or inconsistent?

- What surprised me about my own communication this week?

Week 2

Weekly Focus:

Daily Practice Completed

- Mon ☐ Tue ☐ Wed ☐ Thu ☐ Fri ☐ Sat ☐ Sun ☐

End of Week Reflection

- What improved this week?
- What still feels weak or inconsistent?
- What surprised me about my own communication this week?

Week 3

Weekly Focus:

Daily Practice Completed

- Mon ☐ Tue ☐ Wed ☐ Thu ☐ Fri ☐ Sat ☐ Sun ☐

End of Week Reflection

- What improved this week?
- What still feels weak or inconsistent?
- What surprised me about my own communication this week?

Week 4

Weekly Focus:

Daily Practice Completed

- Mon ☐ Tue ☐ Wed ☐ Thu ☐ Fri ☐ Sat ☐ Sun ☐

End of Week Reflection

- What improved this week?
- What still feels weak or inconsistent?
- What surprised me about my own communication this week?

Final 30-Day Reflection

Complete this on Day 30 after recording and reviewing your final video. Answer each question in full sentences. Do not rush this. It is the most important writing you will do in this entire protocol.

1. What has specifically changed in my communication since Day 1?

2. What have others noticed differently about the way I communicate?

3. Which habit improved the most across these thirty days?

4. What still needs the most refinement going forward?

5. What will my primary focus be in the next thirty day

A Final Word

You have reached the end of this book. But you have not reached the end of this work.

Communication is not a subject you finish. It is a standard you raise — continuously, deliberately, through honest observation and consistent practice. The chapters gave you an understanding. The protocol gave you the structure. This appendix gives you the mirror.

Come back to it. Every thirty days. Every time you feel you have plateaued. Every time a recording surprises you with something you had not noticed before.

The most important thing you can do now is not remember what you read. It is a press record.

Personal Closing Letter

This book did not begin with a writing plan.

It began with a question I could not stop asking: why do so many intelligent, capable people struggle to express what they know?

I spent years trying to answer that question. Not in a classroom, not through a single course, but through continuous study — reading, observing, practising, failing, and refining. I studied communication not as an academic subject but as a living skill. I watched how people spoke under pressure. I noticed what separated those who were heard from those who were overlooked. I tested ideas in real conversations and kept only what actually worked.

Everything inside this book — every framework, every principle, every observation — came from that process. The content was decided, shaped, and prepared by me. The experiences behind it are real. Those years that went into understanding this subject were genuinely mine.

I will be honest with you about one thing. In bringing this material to the page, I worked with the assistance of artificial intelligence to help structure the format, integrate stories, and refine the language. I believe in being transparent about that. AI served as a co-author in the craft of writing this book. But it was never the source of the ideas. It helped me build the house. The architecture was always mine.

This is my first book. My first attempt at taking everything I have learned and putting it into something another person can hold, read, and use. That feels significant to me, and I did not want to reach the final page without saying so.

If even one chapter changed the way you think about communication, this was worth writing.

If one exercise gave you a moment of honest self-awareness, these years were worth spending.

And if you ever feel the work is too slow, the progress too small, or the gap between where you are and where you want to be too wide — return to Chapter 2. Read it again. Remember that discomfort is not a signal to stop.

It is a signal that something is being built.

Thank you for reading.

Author - Shivam Nanda

2026

About the Author

Shivam Nanda is a communication educator, teacher, and content creator with a singular focus: helping students and professionals learn to think clearly, speak confidently, and communicate with genuine impact. Over the course of years of deep study into the science and practice of human communication, Shivam immersed himself in everything from the neuroscience of fear and the physiology of voice to the architecture of storytelling and the psychology of emotional intelligence. What emerged from that process was not just a collection of knowledge but a structured training system — one built on the belief that communication is not a personality trait, but a skill that can be developed by anyone willing to observe themselves honestly and practise deliberately. Through teaching, coaching, and content creation, he has worked with learners across a wide spectrum — from school students finding their voice for the first time to young professionals navigating interviews, presentations, and workplace conversations. His approach has always been the same: remove the mystery, provide the structure, and trust the student to do the work. This book is the most complete expression of that approach to date. It is Shivam's first book — a step-by-step communication mastery manual designed specifically for students and early professionals who are done with vague advice and ready for a practical, honest path forward. He believes, and this book reflects, that the gap between where most people are and where they want to be as communicators is not talent. It is awareness. It is structured. It is the willingness to press record, listen back, and begin again.

You can follow his work on his YouTube channel "Learning Now by Shivam Nanda"

www.ingramcontent.com/pod-product-compliance
Ingram Content Group UK Ltd.
Pitfield, Milton Keynes, MK11 3LW, UK
UKHW041351190726
13845UKWH00026B/540

9 789357 808644